Attic Windows
quilts with a view

Diana Leone & Cindy Walter
2nd Edition

Published by

Krause Publications
700 East State St., Iola, WI 54990-0001
Telephone (715) 445-2214
www.krause.com

Please call or write for our free catalog of publications. Our toll-free number to place an order or obtain a free catalog is 800-258-0929 or please use our regular business telephone 715-445-2214 for editorial comment and further information.

Library of Congress Catalog Number 99-66145
ISBN 0-87341-834-4

Products in this book are registered trademarks of their respective companies:
Clover Flower™
Dream Snipper™
Husqvarna/Viking Designer™ embroidery machine
Marti Michell's Perfect Patchwork™
Patchworkapplique™
Purple Thang™
Touch of Gold™ fusible
True Point™

Most photos in this book by Richard Johns, San Jose, CA, and Kris Kandler, Krause Publications, Iola, WI.

Table of Contents

From the Authors

From Diana

My first Attic Window quilt was Copy Cat. I saw a small, wonderful quilt made by Allegra McIver at a quilt show and it inspired me to make a Copy Cat. Large tropical print fabrics with toucans and leaves made the quilt bright, cheerful, and fun to view. Little did I know that this quilt would inspire me to make many Attic Window quilts and write the first how-to book on Attic Window techniques in 1984.

I began seeing ideas for Attic Window quilts everywhere. While traveling through cities, I observed the illusion of depth in windows created by light on the buildings. I saw little windows, tall windows, painted windows, stained glass windows—windows of every size and shape imaginable. Every window became a quilt possibility.

My enthusiasm for Attic Window quilts has carried over to quilting friends and students, and everyone has made a new Attic Window quilt to share with you. The next step was to share my excitement by bringing you this new book. Today, you will be able to take advantage of the best speed piecing, accurate mitering techniques, current tools, and the many great fabrics that are waiting for you to feature in your own Attic Window quilts.

Cindy Walter had used my first book and knew it was currently out of print. The demand for the book remained high, so Cindy went to Krause Publications and encouraged the company to reissue the book. Cindy has generously co-authored this all-new addition. We are sure you will enjoy seeing the more than 50 full-color Attic Window quilts in this book along with the methods and materials which are updated and available in your area. We hope you will be inspired to make many Attic Window quilts.

Diana Leone

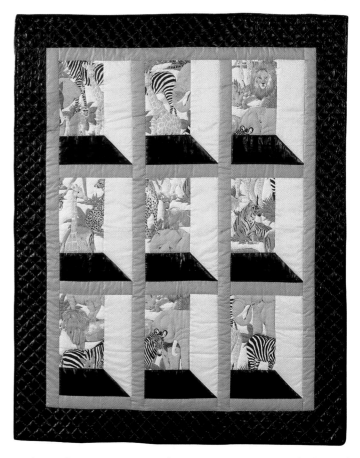

Hank's Quilt, 40" x 58", 1987, by Diana Leone. Diana made this quilt with Concord fabrics for her late father-in-law, Henry Leone.

Fine Hand Quilting, 2nd Edition
and the original Attic Windows.

From Cindy

I have been teaching traditional quilting techniques for many years, and often out of Diana's books. So, working on a project with her is an honor and a learning adventure. We just finished rewriting *Fine Hand Quilting* (I'm sure you will find that book very exciting), and we both still have our wits about us and are able to approach this book with a high level of enthusiasm. I hope you enjoy using our books as much as I've enjoyed writing them.

A special thank you to my family and friends for their constant support. Working on three books in one year has been a challenge that is already full of rewards. The quilts in these books have brought Diana and I new friends and a visual feast we can share with you. And yes, we are planning on writing several books in the future!

Finally, a special thank you to our sponsors, Husqvarna Viking Sewing Machines, Springs—For Quilters Only, Northcott/Monarch Fabric, The Warm Company, and the many manufacturers who willingly shared their fabrics and products for us to use and test and for their endless support to this book.

Cindy Walter

P.S. Coming soon is *More Snippet Sensations*, being released in 2000 from Krause Publications. One of the Snippet projects from this new book is Snippet Garden, featured below.

Snippet Garden, 48" x 60", 1999, by Cindy Walter. Cindy created this beautiful flower garden using her Snippet Sensations technique. Once the flower garden was complete, she divided it into twelve sections to create an Attic Window. The quilt was displayed in the "Quilts in Bloom" exhibit held in the Castle Gallery of the Mainau in Konstance, Germany.

section 1

The Basics

Introduction

Making an Attic Window quilt is a very straightforward process that is a lot of fun and a great way to use your imagination, creativity, and your favorite printed motif fabrics. The Attic Window is a good beginning project for children and adults. The pieces are large and easy to machine assemble. The speed piecing technique we have developed makes the process fast. You will find more fun fabrics than you know what to do with because suitable fabrics for Attic Windows abound. You can use any printed design, or motif, for the theme of the window portion. Printed fabrics, pieced blocks, stenciled fabric, photo transfer, machine embroidered, redwork, or appliqué—almost any motif will work in the window. The design may be as traditional or contemporary as you can imagine. Open the window to your own creativity, and follow along—it is really easy and fun.

Because each of your quilts will vary in size, you will need to determine first the window size, then the width of the sashing and ledge, and finally the desired finished quilt size. Window grid layout patterns are included to help you plan the quilt and estimate the yardage (see pages 30-33). For inspiration, we have noted the window and sashing dimensions for several of the featured quilts in this book. And we have included a step-by-step project using a printed fabric (see page 44). Have fun, and when you are finished, please send us photos of your Attic Window quilts.

Home is Where the Heart Is, 36" x 42", 1999, by Terri Vogds. Mary Engelbreit-designed fabric from VIP was a perfect choice for these windows. The sashing is 1", the ledge ¹/₂", and the window sizes are 8" x 6".

Painted window on a building in Los Altos, CA.

Feathered and Furry Friends, 55¹/₂" x 59", 1998, by Ursula Reikes. For eight years, Ursula photographed animals at the Cougar Mountain Zoo in Issaquah, Washington. She combined the photo transfer technique and batik fabrics to create this lasting memory of a few of her best friends. Note that the 2¹/₂" sashings are strip pieced using a variety of fabrics to add color and texture. This quilt is featured in the book Quilting Your Memories *(TPP), by Sandy Bonsib. Photo by Brent Kane.*

Looking Through a Window: A Simple Exercise

Windows create an opening so you can see the outside while remaining inside the building, enjoying the warmth and comfort of the surroundings. Windows also let you look inside and give you a glimpse of what is going on without intruding. The window sash on Diana's kitchen window is divided into six parts. While getting a cup of coffee one day, she looked out this window and thought of a great exercise to help you "see" a scene for a quilt.

To understand how color, value, scale, depth, and perspective work in a quilt, take a moment to look through a window. Stand inside a room and look outside. You will see a perfect scene for an Attic Window quilt. Look at the overall color and value of the scene. Notice how the colors nearest to you are clearer and brighter; those same colors become more muted, softer, bluer, and grayer when they are farther away. Objects close to the window are large and fill the window. The same object, if farther away, appears smaller. If you are going to include depth and atmospheric value and color change, make a note of these phenomena and let your observations help you determine the scale, color, and value selection for the quilt. Use photographs of your favorite scenes for inspiration.

Safari Sampler, 32" x 32", 1998, by Virginia Rojas. Here, Virginia used three different fabrics to create perspective. Note how the animals at the bottom appear larger, those in the middle row are smaller, and the mountains recede into the distance. Virginia also used a one-point perspective (see page 36) to achieve additional depth.

Supply List

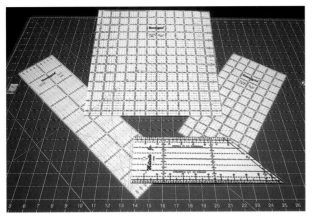

Fabric (see yardage charts, pages 30-33)
Pins (True Point or Clover Flower head)
Scissors (sharp fabric scissors)
Large rotary cutter (with a new, sharp blade)
Large rotary cutting mat
Rotary cutting guide for strip cutting (6″ x 24″ or 6″ x 18″)
Cutting guide for mitered sashing (choose one):
    Omnigrid 6″ x 18″ gridded ruler
    Marti Michell's Perfect Patchwork templates (Set C 1″ wide sashing or Set D 1¼″ sashing)
Cutting guide for sizing blocks (choose one):
    Omnigrid 12½″ or 15″ square
    Two 11″ x 17″ gridded template plastic sheets
Washable pen or pencil
Iron and ironing board
Sewing machine
Walking foot (dual feed foot)
Sewing machine needles, Jeans (Denims), sizes 10 or 11
Thread, high quality, 100-percent cotton
Basting tools (choose one):
    Long Milliner needles and white cotton thread
    Basting gun and tags (tagging gun)
    Safety pins, size 0 or 1
    Quilt Adhesive Spray, 505 or KK 2000
Batting, high quality (thin cotton for machine quilting, thin polyester for hand quilting)
Hand or machine quilting supplies (see pages 62-64)

Components of the Attic Window Quilt

The window piece and two or more sashing pieces make up an Attic Window block. A ledge may be added to frame each block. The border finalizes the scene, and the binding finishes the edges.

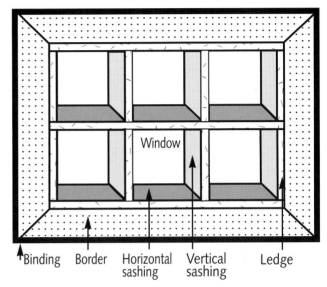

Binding   Border   Horizontal sashing   Vertical sashing   Ledge

Window

The window provides the large focal point which contains the theme of the quilt. The windows may be any size and may even be different sizes within one quilt. The window portion may be printed fabric, pieced, an appliquéd or stenciled block, or may be constructed in any way you desire. Each window contributes to the overall design theme of the quilt, yet by itself it may be one piece of art. For example, if the quilt has a tropical theme, fabric motifs used in the windows might be palm trees, surfers, and a sunset. When you have "composed" and sewn all of the different windows together, you create the tropical scene.

Sashing

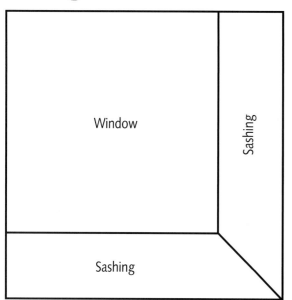

The sashing is the framing strip sewn to the edge of the window. If two sashings of equal width are sewn to adjacent sides of the window, the joining seam is a 45° miter. The mitered seam enhances the window effect. The sashing may be sewn on two, three, or four sides of the window. If you use a perspective view, the sashing width and the degree of the miter's angle will vary. It is the contrast of the three values used for the window and sashing at the 45° miter seam that creates the depth.

The width of the sashing is usually one-third, or less, of the window's width. Feel free to experiment with the width of the sashing. Note that different widths create different effects.

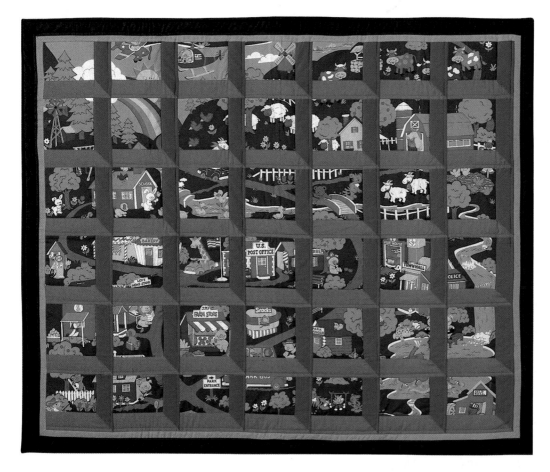

Play Time View, 58" x 47", 1988, by Martha Meyer. This quilt was machine pieced and hand quilted using a V.I.P. children's print. Martha used a sashing width that was about one-third of the window size.

Ledge

The ledge is a narrow strip of fabric that frames the window and sashing. These narrow fabric strips, which are optional, add an additional level of depth to the scene. The ledge unifies and separates busy windows. A very light value emphasizes depth. The ledge's width is usually one-third, or less, of the sashing's width. Feel free to experiment with its width to create the desired effect. The ledge's value is usually very light or very dark.

City Lights, 40" x 44", 1999, by Diana Leone. Diana was inspired to make this quilt to the celebrate the new millennium using Fabric Traditions New Millennium fabrics. Diana designed the "Rain and Mist" fabrics used for the ledge, sashing, and border for Northcott/Monarch in 1999. The silver metallic made the "Rain" fabric the perfect choice to coordinate with the city skyline's night scene. The finished sashing is 1³/₄" wide, and the ledge is ¹/₄" wide.

Border

The border is made up of strips added to the perimeter of the assembled inner quilt top. In addition to extending the final dimensions of the quilt top, the border can further enhance the apparent depth of the windows, providing a frame to encapsulate the scene. The border also provides an area in which to include some creative hand or machine quilting. Any number of borders can be added, and they can be any width needed to make the quilt the desired finished size.

Binding

The binding is the edge sewn around the quilt's perimeter to encase the raw edges of the quilt's layers (see page 66). Any color or print fabric can be used as the binding. A darker fabric is most often used to finalize the edge.

MicAsh's Range, 30" x 40", 1999, by Lynn Whitson Carrico. Lynn was inspired to make this quilt for her son-in-law, Michael, because of the many trips she would take to his and her daughter's home. While there, she would often stand and look out into the field at the horses the two raise. The Alexander Henry boot fabric is a perfect border, combining the theme with a little humor.

Selecting Fabrics for the Windows

Panel or Printed Fabric

You can use one printed theme panel fabric for all of the windows, combine theme panels and theme coordinates, or use many different prints together in one quilt. We are in an era when excellent and exciting fabrics are being printed, and suitable printed fabrics for Attic Window quilts are available in great abundance. You will find large, small, cute, sophisticated, and every kind of "theme" print ready for your use. Whatever your first idea or theme may be, leave a little room for creative decision-making at the fabric store. In selecting fabrics, you are building the palette with which you will paint the scene in the Attic Window quilt.

Detail from Susan Kinkki's California Classics.

California Classics, 38" x 42", 1993, by Susan Kinkki. I wonder who those guys are. Could the body boarder be George Greeno, and the surfers Jerry Lopez or the Hoffman brothers? Finding the theme fabric took on a special meaning for Susan, who lives in Hawaii. Some of the "sufers" came from old shirts and a few others from retro fabrics.

Wolf Pack, 46" x 54", 1999, by Cindy Walter. Cindy was inspired to make this quilt after seeing a great panel fabric (shown below) from Springs Industries, Inc. She used a variety of window sizes to showcase the different fabric motifs. Private collection of Frank Hulce.

Composing

Using a Variety of Coordinating Theme Prints

Composing a scene using various printed fabrics is somewhat spontaneous: you visualize the scene, make some sketches, select the fabrics, and lay them out before you begin. Creating a scene from multiple fabrics often requires trial and error. You may find numerous motifs in a yard of printed fabric, or you may need 2 yards to cut enough motifs for even a small quilt. It is the print, the size of the print, and the combination of prints that will make your visual statement. The different prints' background values (the lightness to darkness) and the prints' size (scale) will affect the illusion of depth. Use lighter values near the top and darker values at the bottom to add to the illusion of depth.

Winter Charm, 31" x 31", 1999, Joanna Schneider. Joanna created this quilt as a memory and fantasy of her hometown in Pennsylvania during the wintertime. She used two different fabrics for the windows. The sashing is 1¹/₂", the ledge is ¹/₂", and the windows are 6" x 6". Collect your holiday fabrics during the time of year they appear in the quilt shop; set them aside for that rainy day of quilt making. Collect panels of prints, because they provide good resources for Attic Windows.

Application of Value, Color, and Scale

Here are a few simplified suggestions about value, color, and scale that we have found to work and that may help in your fabric selection.

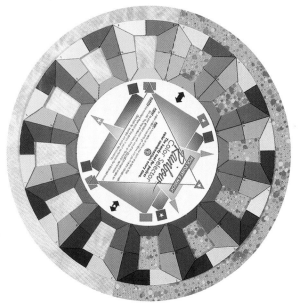

This Rainbow Color Selector shows the contrast of color value.

Value

Value is the lightness or darkness of color. Its range can be established from light to dark by observing the tints, tones, and shades of each color. For example, with the color blue, light blue is a tint (white added) and navy is a shade (black added). Light tints will come forward and darker shades will recede. Tone is color with gray added, or "dusty" colors: dusty blue is a tone (gray added). Tones are mostly mid-range in value. Many values of blue can be found between these extremes, depending on how much white, black, or gray is combined with the blue.

Light to dark.

Variety of values.
Above: Darks
Right: Mediums
Below: Brights, dark, light, and medium

Dark values and colors contrast with the theme fabric.

Value is the first element in achieving contrast. An effective Attic Window illusion is achieved by contrasting the parts of the window block (window, sashing, and ledge). Contrast is achieved in many ways: you will use value and color contrasts, combined with the contrast of scale and size, to create depth in the window. How you contrast the value of the window fabric with the value of the sashing fabric will determine how close or how far away the window scene will appear.

Medium light values and color contrast are used to achieve the illusion of depth.

Autumn Windows, 84" x 96", 1999, Laura Munson Reinstatler. Peggy and Randy Schafer commissioned this quilt, which is based on a dried-flower wall hanging by French artist Elizabeth Helm. The 6" block is a variation of the Spool block, but the color and value placement create the Attic Window effect. Approximately 150 fabrics from the Color Reference Library by Benartex, Inc. contribute a rich variety of hues and textures. Laura speed-cut the pieces on Alto's QuiltCut Fabric Cutting System. Private collection of Peggy and Randy Schafer.

Notice how the higher contrast sashing makes the center square appear further away.

Notice how the lower contrast sashing makes the block appear flat with no illusion of depth.

Value of the Window Fabric

If you use one fabric for all of the windows, determine the fabric's general value. Select the sashing to contrast with the overall value of the fabric's background.

Light   Medium   Dark

Great examples of light, medium, and dark windows. Details from Lynn Whitson Carrico's MicAsh's Range (see page 12 for full quilt).

If you are combining, or "composing," and using many different fabrics for the windows, they may all have different backgrounds, so consider them to be all one value. If you could place all of the window fabrics in a paint pot and stir them up, what would the overall value be? You must decide whether they are mostly light, medium, dark, or somewhere in between.

Detail of Terri Vogds' Friends in the Attic. The center blocks average to become a medium value.

Value of the Sashing Fabric

The sashing fabrics frame the window fabrics and create a grid over the window scene. The visual effect of depth is created by a strong contrasting value where the vertical and horizontal sashes meet at the miter seam. You will be able to see how the contrast-ing value of the sashing fabrics works together with the window fabrics if you "paste up" the fabrics on a layout grid. Use your light, medium, and dark fabric combination and paste up a window block to see if the contrast of the fabrics' values works together to achieve depth.

Friends in the Attic, 30" x 30", 1999, by Terri Vogds. The blocks for this quilt were made by the Denton Quilt Guild during a year-long 4" block exchange. Terri pieced the top and machine quilted it when the exchange was finished. When a combination of blocks is used together, finding the best value to contrast the blocks may require some trial and error. Usually a higher contrast (light and dark fabric with a "non-print") is best for the sashing in the project. Notice how the narrow, high contrast (very dark) ledge fabric adds to the depth. A light and a dark valued fabrics were chosen for the sashing as a good contrast to the "medium" windows.

• More depth: If the window fabrics are mostly a light value, use one medium and one dark fabric for the adjacent sashings to achieve greater depth.

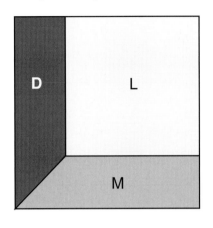

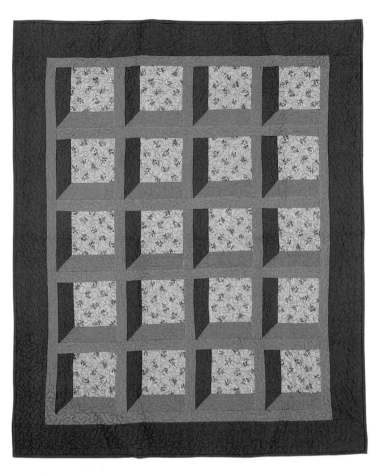

A Teal Day, 32" x 38", 1999, by Connie Draper, machine quilted by Cindy Walter. Because Connie lives on her family farm and is very busy in the summer, she enjoys quilt making as a winter pastime. Connie pieced this simple but beautiful wall hanging, which Cindy, her niece, quilted. This quilt showcases a light window with a medium and dark sashing.

• More depth: If the window fabrics are mostly a dark value, use one light and one medium fabric for the two sashings to achieve greater depth.

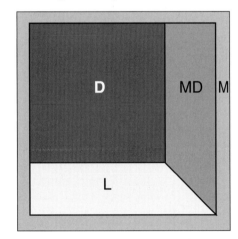

Sun Bonnet Sue, 28" x 28", 1999, by Diana Leone. Diana used photo transfer images from Moonstone Creations for the quilt's windows. The original images are from a set of postcards produced in 1907. Diana Leone designed all of the other fabrics for Northcott/Monarch.

- More depth: If the window fabrics are mostly a medium value, use one light and one dark value fabric for the two sashings to achieve greater depth.

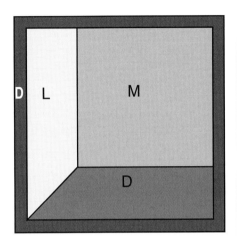

Go!, 36" x 42", 1999, by Olga Bratkovskaia. The sport-themed fabric was perfect for the large window in the middle of this quilt, which she made for her 7-year-old son. Notice how the thin black lattice separates the busy blocks.

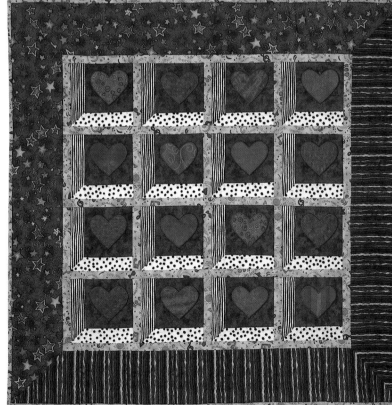

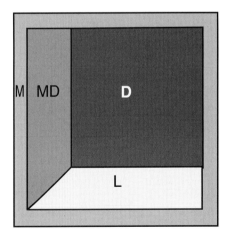

Hearts in the Attic, 40" x 40", 1999, Terri Vogds. Terri made many hand and machine appliquéd blocks. The Attic Window pattern provided a perfect framework in which to feature her small treasures. The very light and medium sashes are the best choice to contrast with the dark window blocks.

- Less depth: If the window fabrics are mostly a dark value, use one medium and one dark sashing fabric for a closer view.

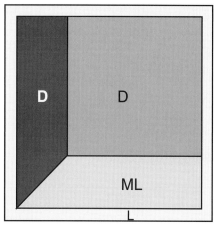

Windows into the Eighteenth Dynasty, 32" x 32", 1999, by Joanna Schneider. Joanna used Timeless Treasures' Egyptian-themed fabric to create the motif in the windows. For an interesting touch, she used a gradating green fabric from Benartex Inc. for the sashing.

- Less depth: If the window fabrics are mostly a medium value, use one medium/dark and one light fabric for the sashings to achieve a close view.

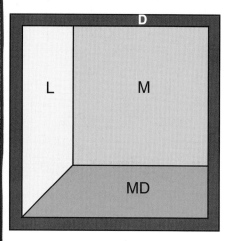

Windows of Wildlife, 70" x 72", 1998, by Kristina Wallace. Kristina lives in the beautiful northwestern United States, with the Olympic Mountains nearby. Her inspiration for this, her first quilt, came from camping and hiking in these mountains.

Value of the Ledge Fabric

Some of the quilts in this book include a strip of fabric sewn vertically and horizontally between the window blocks; we call this part of the quilt the ledge. The value of the ledge fabric enhances the illusion of depth and separates busy windows. A strong contrast in value between the ledge fabric and the sashing fabric is best. Select the ledge fabric following these guidelines:

- A light ledge gives the effect of a light shining on the edge of a real window. A light ledge will come forward and will make it look as though you are outside looking in.

- A dark ledge acts as a framework and will make it seem as though you are looking out from the inside.

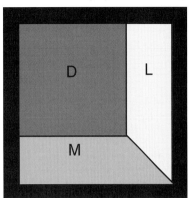

Notice that the ledges are very dark. The dark border acts as a final frame around the scene.

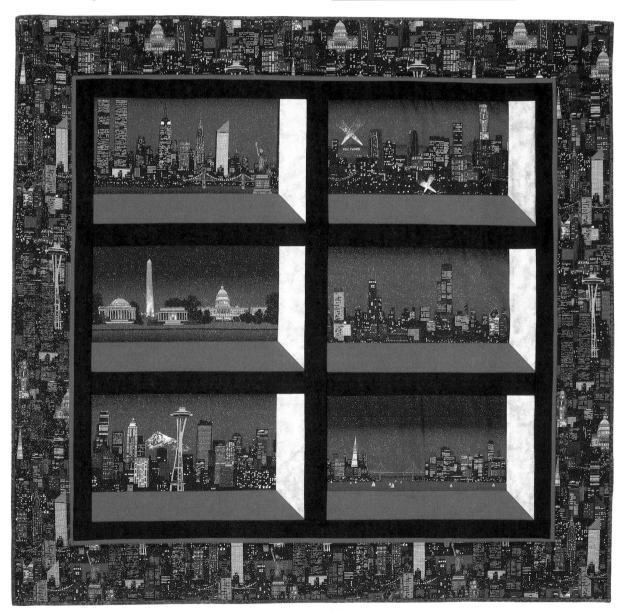

Seattle Alli, Millennium, 42" x 40", 1999, by Dawna Callahan. Because she works at a quilt shop in Bellevue, Washington, Dawna sees new fabric as it arrives in the shop. She couldn't resist making an Attic Window from this fabric by Fabric Traditions, featuring the Seattle skyline.

Color

The fabric used for the sashing and border becomes a dominant color statement. For example, if you want a blue quilt, select blue for the sashing or border.

Blue and Purple Cats, 28" x 28", 1999, by Diana Morrison, machine quilted by Cindy Walter. Diana participated in an Attic Window workshop with Cindy Walter. She wanted her quilt to be primarily blue, so Cindy suggested using the blue fabric in the ledge area. Instead, Diana used the blue fabric as part of the sashing because it looked great with the yellow sashing and purple fabric for the ledge. The quilt became purple because the ledge color was overwhelming. Diana went home and pieced a second quilt overnight using the blue fabric in the ledge area and purple fabric in the sashing; she achieved her desire for a "blue" quilt.

The sashing color does not have to exactly match any color in the window; it is actually better if the sashings' colors contrast with each other and with the window's color than blend into the value of the window fabric. It is also better if the ledge and border colors contrast with each other and with the overall value of the window block. Select lighter or darker values of the colors in the window fabric for the sashing, ledge, and border to enhance and complement the window.

Use color to set the mood and to coordinate with the area where the quilt will be displayed. Warm colors, such as red, yellow, and orange, tend to come forward and make you think of the daytime, sun, and warmth. Cool colors, like blue, green, and violet, make you think of nighttime, snow, and the cold—these generally recede into the distance. Bright, clear colors will come forward, while grayed colors recede. We pasted-up our parrot fabric and tested different sashing colors until we found the right combination that fit that tropic mood we were trying to create (see page 40).

Use black and white carefully. Black will create a hole or lifeless area, so instead of black, try a very dark green, burgundy, or navy. Also, think about using off-white or a lighter tint of a color rather than stark-white as a blank area.

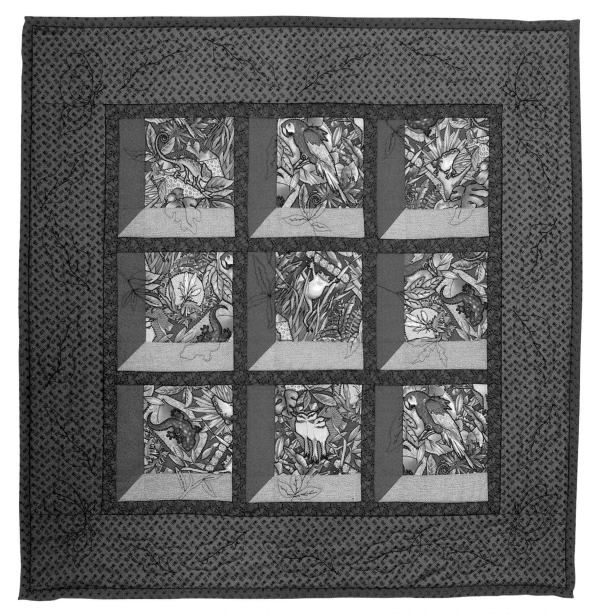

A Wilder View of Life, 37" x 37", 1999, by Francine Beanan. Francine used Rain Forest, by H. Kaufman Fabrics, to make this stunning quilt. The use of "crayon" color brights makes this cheerful quilt suitable for any child's room.

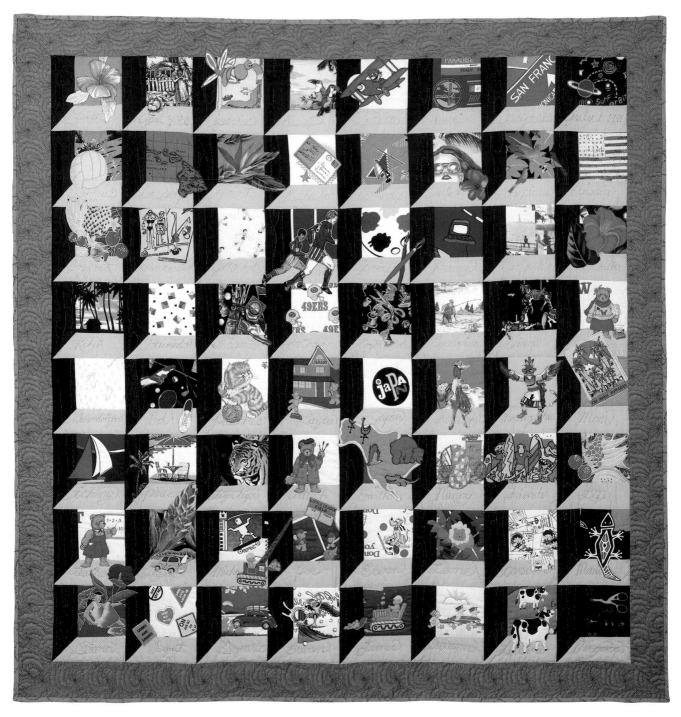

Memories, 80" x 80", 1987, by Diana Leone. This quilt is full of memories from Diana's life. Some of the fabrics date from the 1960s and '70s; each represents a friend or activity in her life. Notice the appliqué pieces that continue over the sashings; they seem to come alive and walk out of the window. The larger prints come forward and the smaller prints seem to be further in the distance. Diana developed this original technique of patchworkappliqué in 1987 (see page 80) for a close-up view. Neutral, light-valued fabrics were used as the sashing in this multi-motif Attic Window quilt. Black and gray sashes help showcase the variety of prints and colors in Diana's favorite things-themed quilt.

Scale

"Scale" is the size of the print. Scale is always relative, meaning something's "scale" is only what it is when compared to something else. The size of the print in relationship to the size of the window will enhance or lessen the illusion of depth in the window. Generally, small prints will recede and large prints will come forward.

The fabric motifs, depending on the size of the print, may repeat several times within a yard. There may be hundreds of little flowers repeated in a yard or as few as one to four large flowers. Keep the following in mind while choosing prints:

- If the print is small and you want it to appear far away, use a print that shows a lot of background.
- If the print is small and you want it to appear close, use a small window. Let the print fill the window to appear closer.
- If you use a large print with little background that fills the window area, it will appear close.
- If the print is large and you want it to appear far away, use a large window and make sure some background is showing.

Small print

Small print

Small print

Medium print

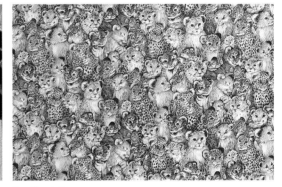

Medium

Large print

Large

Road to Hana Bay, by Diana Leone, has large windows which gave her room to create a theme quilt with the very large-scale fabric. The water area recedes because the motifs are smaller and some background shows in the windows. It is not easy to show depth when the background colors and values vary in one quilt and when the prints vary from large to small. When the elements vary in scale and value, don't worry about it; the end result will be just fine.

The windows at the top of the quilt Hawaii, Hawaii, by Diana Leone (on page 74), appear to be farther away because more background appears around each print. The idea of the sky, sea, and land was used to place the window from top to bottom. Prints fill the windows in some areas of the quilt, bringing those windows closer to the viewer. A medium and a dark blue were used as sashing colors to unify the complicated, busy windows.

Road to Hana Bay, 108" x 90", 1988, by Diana Leone. The quilt's large windows gave Diana room to create the scene with larger-scale fabrics. The water area recedes because the motifs are smaller and some background shows in the windows. Diana made this quilt for her son, Joe, who loves to travel, surf, and ski. Neutral blue and gray fabrics were used for the 3" sashing. The use of a neutral sashing helps calm down the busier prints.

Patches and Xanadu Are Watching, 30" x 40", 1987, by Diana Leone. Diana used cat pillow panels and cat fabrics. This quilt features a light background with medium/dark and medium sashings. Notice the use of the brown and gray for the sashing; neither color "exactly" matches the prints, yet the neutrals effectively provide a complementary color scheme to the various cat fabrics. Note how the smaller cats recede and the larger ones jump forward.

Yardage Requirements

Because of the many variables in creating an Attic Window quilt, our yardage estimates are ample and, in most cases, are more than you will need. The estimates allow for seaming and shrinkage. Use the leftover fabrics for a creatively pieced back or another project.

Pre-wash the fabrics without using soap (or you can use a phosphate-free quilt soap such as Orvus quilt soap), to remove excess sizing, dyes, and set shrinkage. Leave the selvage on while washing to help prevent frayed edges. Remove the selvages before cutting the pattern pieces (the selvages are too dense to sew and quilt through). Press the fabric as needed.

Use the diagrams included with each quilt size or the layout designs on pages 34 and 35 to help plan your quilt.

Wall Quilts

Many quilters quickly cover all of the beds they can find with quilts and then go "onto the wall." The Attic Window is one of the most suitable designs for a wall quilt because it is visually graphic and an appealing quilt to view in any setting. You can easily add a piece of "fabric art" to any room or office by making a personalized Attic Window.

A wall quilt that is approximately 41" wide by 48" high is a manageable size (if you stay under 41" wide, you only need one length of fabric for the backing). For example, use these finished measurements:

Finished quilt: 41" width, 48" height
Windows: 4 across, 3 down
Window size: 5" width, 7" height
Sashing: 2" wide
Ledge: 1" wide
Borders: 4" wide

Wall Quilt

Window size:	
Cut 4" x 4" to 8" x 10"	1 fabric, small print: $1\frac{1}{2}$ yards or,
	1 fabric, large print: 2 yards or,
	2 or more fabrics: $\frac{3}{4}$ yard each (2 yards total)
Sashing width:	
Cut 2" to 3" wide	2 fabrics: $\frac{3}{4}$ yard each
Ledge width:	
Cut 1" to $1\frac{1}{2}$"	1 fabric: $1\frac{1}{2}$ yards
Border:	
5" wide or less	1 fabric: $1\frac{3}{4}$ yards
Backing:	
42" wide x 60" long	1 fabric: $1\frac{7}{8}$ yards
Binding:	
Cut $2\frac{3}{4}$" wide	1 fabric: $\frac{3}{4}$ yard
Cut $1\frac{1}{2}$" wide	1 fabric: $\frac{1}{2}$ yard

Wall quilt with ledge.

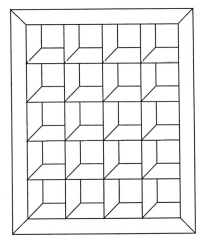

Wall quilt with no ledge.

Bed Quilts

Design the Attic Window block section (inner top) to fit the top of the bed. Add the borders to make the finished quilt the size desired. Calculate the dimensions on the following layout designs that correspond with the size you intend to make. Make photocopies of the layout design (see page 34), then cut and paste the photocopies together as needed to make the final configuration.

Your quilt will become slightly smaller when it is quilted. If you want the quilt to be an exact size, measure the width and length of the bed using a tape measure. Add 2″ to the width and length for a twin bed to allow for the quilting and add up to 6″, to the length and width, to a king bed measurement to allow for quilting. These are estimates; each of your quilts will vary, but it is better to have some extra yardage than not enough. The excess fabric can always be trimmed away.

Detail from Cecile Jaffrennou and June Jones' A Year in a Bear's Life (see page 93 for full quilt).

Twin/Single

Bed top or window area: 40″ to 65″
Finished size with 10″ border: 60″ x 85″
Finished size with 20″ border: 80″ x 105″
Measure the bed to determine the needed size. If the border is wider than 10″, purchase two lengths of border fabric.

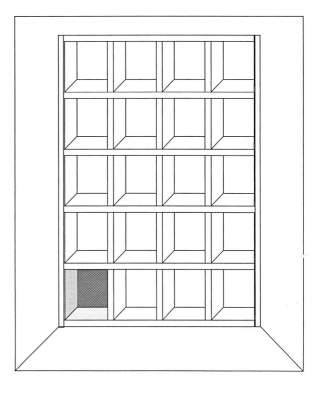

Window size:	
Cut 4″ x 6″ to 8″ x 11″	1 fabric, small print: 2 yards or,
	1 fabric, large print: 3 yards or,
	2 or more fabrics: 3 yards total
Sashing width:	
Cut 1″ to 3″ wide	2 fabrics: 1 yard each or,
	3 or 4 fabrics: $1/2$-$3/4$ yard each
	(2 yards total)
Ledge width:	
Cut 1″ to 2″	1 fabric: $2^{1}/2$ yards
Border:	
11″ wide or less	1 fabric: 3 yards
12″ wide or more	1 fabric: 6 yards
Backing:	
2 widths (42″ x 108″)	$6^{1}/2$ yards
Binding:	
Cut $2^{3}/4$″ wide	1 fabric: $1^{1}/4$ yards
Cut $1^{1}/2$″ wide	1 fabric: $3/4$ yard

Double

Bed top or window area: 54″ x 72″
Finished size with 10″ border: 74″ x 92″
Finished size with 20″ border: 94″ x 112″

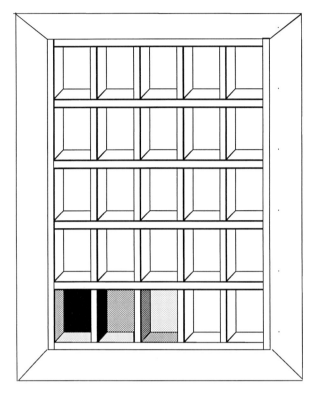

Window size:		
Cut 5″ x 7″ to 10″ x 14″	1 fabric, small print: 4 yards or,	
	1 fabric, large print: 5 yards or,	
	2 or more fabrics: 5 yards total	
Sashing width:		
Cut 1″ to 3″ wide	2 fabrics: 1½ yards each or,	
	3 or 4 fabrics: 1½ yards each (2 yards total)	
Ledge width:		
Cut 1″ to 3″	1 fabric: 2¾ yards	
Binding:		
Cut 2¾″ wide	1 fabric: 1½ yards	
Cut 1½″ wide	1 fabric: 1 yard	
Border:		
11″ wide or less	1 fabric: 3¼ yards	
12″ wide or more	1 fabric: 6½ yards	
Backing:		
2 widths (42″ x 98″)	74″ by 98″: 6 yards or,	
3 widths (42″ x 120″)	94″ x 112″: 10 yards	

(You will have leftover backing fabric. Plan ahead and use some of the backing in the quilt top.)

Detail from Susan Marcia Arrow's Spring at Shinn Pond (see page 70 for full quilt).

Queen

Queen: Use the King yardage chart below.
Bed top (window area): 60″ x 80″
Finished size with 10″ border: 80″ x 100″
Finished size with 20″ border: 100″ x 120″

King

Bed top (window area): 72″ x 84″
Finished size: 15″ border: 102″ x 114″
Finished size, with 24″ border (sides and bottom, 24″
    top 8″): 116″ x 128″
Measure the bed to determine the desired finished size.

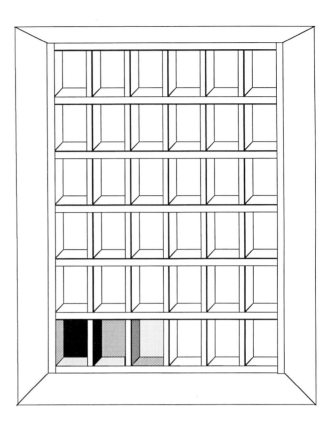

Window size:	
Cut 5″ x 7″ to 12″ x 16″	1 fabric, small print: 5 yards or,
	1 fabric, large print: 7 yards or,
	2 or more fabrics: 7 yards total
Sashing width:	
Cut 1″ to 3″ wide	2 fabrics: 2½ yards each or,
	3 or 4 fabrics: 2 yards each (4 yards total)
Ledge width:	
Cut 1″ to 3″	1 fabric: 2½ yards
Binding:	
Cut 2¾″ wide	1 fabric: 1½ yards
Cut 1½″ wide	1 fabric: 1 yard
Border:	
24″ wide	1 fabric: 7 yards
Backing:	
3 widths	6 yards (10½ yards for quilts wider than 90″)

(You will have leftover backing fabric. Plan ahead and
use some of the backing in the quilt top.)

Detail from Diana Leone's Road to Hana Bay (see page 28 for full quilt).

Layout Diagram

Use this diagram to plan the quilt. Photocopy this page. Cut and paste the copies into the design configuration needed. Write the finished dimensions or measurements on the diagram. Check the yardage requirements and determine what fabric you will need.

The contrast is achieved with value or color contrast. A value or color contrast must be apparent at the miter angle. Paste the window and sashing fabric in the window block pattern. These hints might help you:

• If the window fabric is of light value, use a medium and a dark sashing fabric.
• If the window fabric is of medium value, choose a dark and a light sashing.
• If the window fabric is dark, choose a medium and a light sashing.

Paste-up Page

Use this page to paste pieces of the selected fabric onto the different parts of the Attic Window pattern. You will be able to see how the value of the sashings contrasts with the window fabric. Try different combinations in the different window blocks. If you are using a ledge fabric around the window blocks, also paste this fabric to the grid.

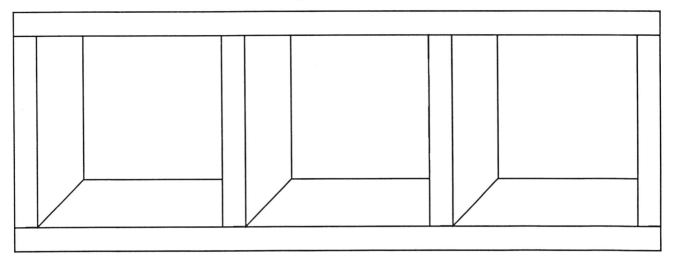

4" Window Pattern

Use this pattern to make a sample Attic Window block to help you visualize the overall design of your quilt. If you are adding a ledge to your quilt, add a ledge to this sample design block also. Sew this little sample block together. You will have a great block to frame and keep as your first Attic Window quilt!

Enlarge or reduce patterns to your desired size.

4" Window Pattern
(5 1/2" finished block)

Add 1/4" seam allowance to all pattern pieces

Use this pattern to make a sample window block

Innovative and Advanced Perspectives in Attic Window Quilts

One-point Perspective

A one-point perspective is created when all of the parallel lines diminish and converge at one point (the vanishing point) on a horizon line within the picture plane. When used in an Attic Window quilt, it adds more dimension to the scene. A one-point perspective is created when a dot (the vanishing point) is placed anywhere within the format of the scene. One horizontal line, parallel to the bottom line, extends to the outside edges from the dot. This line is the horizon line. All lines will converge to the central vanishing point. Notice in Attic Window With a View (on the opposite page) that the artist created a one-point perspective from the center dot.

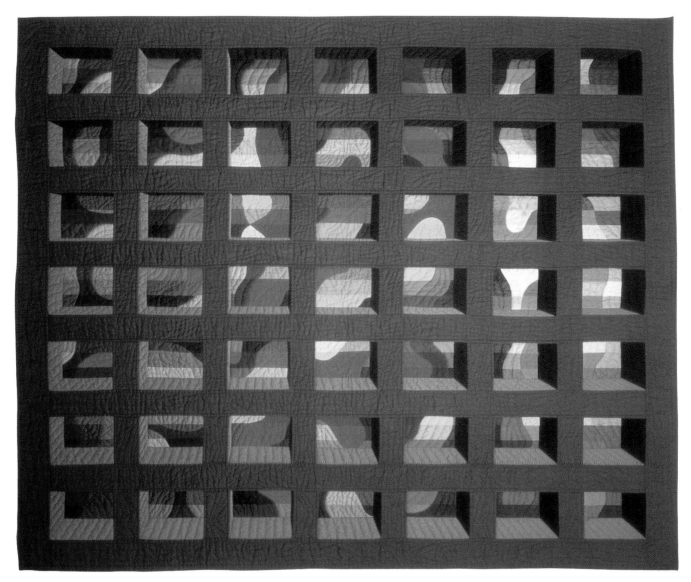

Art Perspectives, 60" x 72", 1984, by Caryl Bryer Fallert. Caryl wanted to create a grid of three-dimensional windows over an abstract landscape. She chose an autumn landscape, because those are her favorite colors, and used a one-point perspective that is below the right center. She drew the quilt full-size to draft the templates for the sashing and the curved landscape pieces in the windows.

One-point Perspective in the Center

Determine the widths of the sashing using one-point perspective with a mid-horizon line in a six-window quilt. The sashing widths will graduate from narrow to wide from the center (the vanishing point) to the edges. The angle of the miter for the sashing will vary. A template will be made for each different sashing (see Sashing, Non-45 Miter, page 52).

Exercise

* Draw a square or a rectangle; divide it into the appropriate number of windows.
* Calculate it so each window is one square inch. (For example, if the project is three windows across by three windows down, the square will be 3" x 3".)
* Place a dot in the middle window.

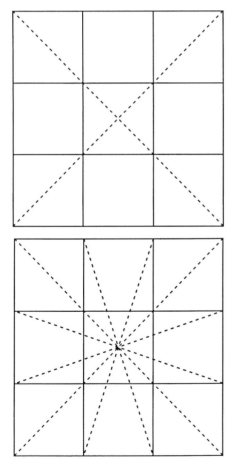

* Using a ruler or straight edge, draw a line through the center dot to each of the four corners. Then draw lines from the center to the corners of each window.
* Starting with the center box, draw the vertical and horizontal lines representing the sashing in each box.

Attic Window With a View, 29" x 29", 1999, by Francine Beanan. Francine used the scenic Diane Phalen fabric by Maywood Studios Eesco to illustrate her use of the point perspective from the center. Notice that the view is made without using a ledge piece.

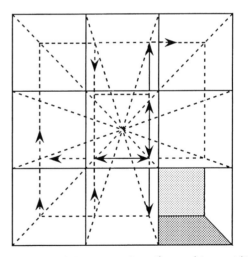

In a one-point perspective, the sashing width and angle of the miter will vary. The sashing in the center is the thinnest, with the sashing in the outer box being the widest.

* Continue drafting lines representing the sashing. Observe that the center window has four sashings, while the others have two or three.
* Use this drawing as a guideline to create the templates you will need to make this quilt. Enlarge the various blocks to the finished size. Remember to add a seam allowance.

Multiple Windows With Non-centered One-point Perspective

The vanishing point is placed above, below, to the right, or to the left of the center. The sashings will graduate from narrow to wide from the vanishing point to the outer edges. Observe that the angle of the miter changes from 45°. Make a template for each different sashing to mark the non-45° angles.

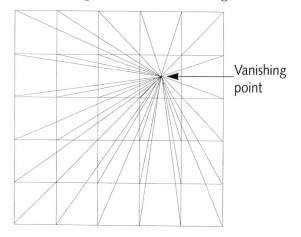

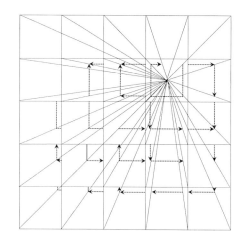

Vanishing point

- Place a dot in the center of one of the blocks. Select a block that is not in the center.
- Draw lines from the vanishing point to the corners of each block. Draw one line from the outer corners of each block to the vanishing point. The blocks that are in the same row as the block with the vanishing point will have a line from two corners to the vanishing point.

- Draw the first vertical line ¹⁄₁₆″ in from the left-hand side of the block with the vanishing point. Draw horizontal and vertical lines connecting the dots where the horizontal and vertical lines touch the angle lines to create different sashing widths.
- You have drafted a plan for a non-centered, one-point perspective Attic Window quilt. See how many different Attic Window quilts you can draft and design.

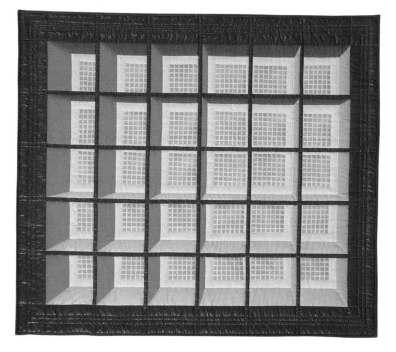

Perspective View, 45" x 58", 1988, by June Inouye. This quilt took a lot of planning; the perspective is from the top right corner. This quilt follows the non centered one point perspective plan. Notice the sashing colors also change to emphasize the illusion of depth.

Creating the Attic Window Quilt

Creating the Quilt Top

Follow these steps to sew an Attic Window quilt together. Review the steps in this section before beginning to sew.

- Cut out all of the parts, including the windows, sashings, ledge, and border using a rotary cutter, cutting guide, and rotary mat.
- Sew the sashings to the window pieces and form the mitered corner.
- If you are using a ledge, add the vertical ledge pieces and sew the horizontal blocks together into rows. Then, add the horizontal ledge strips.
- Sew the rows together.
- If you are using a ledge, add the additional strip around all of the edges as the first, or inner, border.
- Add the border.
- Baste the layers together.
- Quilt by hand or machine.
- Bind and enjoy.

Diana developed the following Attic Window fast piecing method more than 20 years ago. She also developed a few simple sewing techniques to ensure a perfectly squared top. The assembly of the quilt goes together with ease when the pieces are marked and cut accurately. Use a gridded rotary cutting guide to cut the window pieces and to recut the window blocks after all of the blocks are pieced and pressed. The sashing, ledge, and borders are made by measuring, marking, and cutting long strips of fabrics. The windows and sashing are chain pieced, making the process easy and fast. We recommend using a gridded cutting guide, mat, and rotary cutter throughout the quilt making process. Use scissors for small cuts and for all of the cutting if you do not have rotary equipment.

The construction process is shown in detail in the following pages. For a perfectly pieced top, follow each step carefully.

Select, Mark, and Cut Windows

Make the Window Template

Use a clear, large, grid-cutting guide (approx. 15″ x 15″) for measuring and as a window-cutting guide. The fabric motifs can be seen through the plastic, which will help you select what part of the fabric to cut.

Measure and mark the window measurement on the cutting guide. Using ¹/₄″ masking tape, tape along two, or all four, sides of the window measurement's outer edge to represent the seam line and seam allowance. The inside edge of the taped window template will be the finished size of the window. Use this "template" to find the motif on the fabrics and also use the outside edge as a guide to cut the fabric.

Select Windows

Some fabrics may be printed so that you can select and cut in a very straightforward manner (from edge to edge).

This fabric can be cut into window sections without waste.

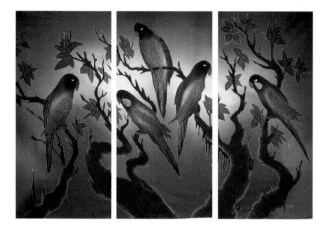

Other fabrics may be printed in such a way that you may have to cut the window right out of the fabric's middle. A printed motif on the fabric may be repeated every few inches or as far apart as 24″. One yard of fabric can yield many similar printed motifs or as few as one to four, depending on how the print is repeated.

To find the "picture" for the window, position four sheets of typing paper around a printed motif. Decide on the window size that best showcases the majority of the motifs in the fabric. If the fabric is an all-over, large-scale print with motifs that are sparsely spaced, begin positioning the template anywhere you "see" your first window.

Cutting the first window may take some courage, because we are not used to cutting a hole in the middle of a fabric piece. You will have the same amount of fabric left over whether you cut a window from the center or edge of the fabric; you just won't be able to make a shirt with the leftover yardage!

With the fabric right side up on a flat surface, place the window template over the first printed motif or design you select.

It is best to position the straight edge of the template on the fabric's horizontal or vertical grain. Occasionally, for a particular positioning, you may have to cut a motif on the fabric's bias. It is all right to cut bias-edged windows; simply cut the piece carefully and take caution not to stretch the window's edges when sewing them to the sashing fabric.

How to Connect Lines in the Window Scene

As you cut more windows and begin to construct the scene, you may begin to see "visual connecting lines." These are areas or lines in the print that appear as though they are connected behind the grid of the sashings and will maintain the scene's visual continuity. The ¹/₂" seam allowance will be consumed in the two seams, bringing the fabrics and prints closer together. Because of this, when a motif has lines that need to connect from one window to the next, you might need to cut parts from two identical prints to achieve the visual continuity. Plan ahead and feature the focal point inside of a window.

If a face or head is to be featured in a window, begin with that part of the fabric and build around it. The Merry Christmas quilts at right are from a printed panel. In the quilt on the right, notice that the face is not as well featured as it is in the other. This quilt was made first and taught the maker to first feature the face and build around it.

- Place the first cut window, right side up, next to the area on the fabric you will cut for the second window.

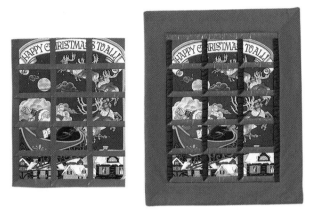

Merry Christmas, 30" x 27", 1988, by Joanne Cranfield. Joanne made the quilt on the right first. While experimenting with the same panel a second time, she found it better to start with Santa's face and work out from there; the face is more centered in the window on the quilt at left. Two panels were used so the lines of the designs would connect and not be lost in the seam allowances.

- Place the gridded plastic window template over the second window. Mark around the template and cut out the window. In order to "see" how the prints will connect, place a strip of sashing fabric between the two cut windows.
- Place each cut window next to the fabric motif to be cut. Overlap the seam allowances and connect the "design lines." Mark each window and continue cutting until there are enough windows for the quilt.
- Label the windows. Mark in the seam allowance on the backside of each block in the horizontal rows. For example, top row left to right, R1 (1), R1 (2), etc., R2 (1), R2 (2), etc. Do not pin the label on the seam line or it will be in your way.

Flying Free, 46" x 65", 1987, by Cathy Risso. Cathy made this quilt for her son, Anthony. It took some thought and planning to select, mark, and cut all of the windows; they are multi-sized and include printed panel fabrics. Notice the hand-appliquéd duck in the upper corner. The hand quilting echoes the print motifs in each window.

aw TIP *Use the Creative Grid, a gridded flannel designed by Diana Leone for ESCO (EESchenck), to use as a design wall. Pin the gridded flannel to a wall and cut the fabric pieces. The pieces will stick to the flannel with no pinning! Play and compose the scene, then remove the fabric pieces and sew the quilt.*

To Compose With One or More Printed Fabrics

Several fabrics, or simply one fabric, can be combined to compose the quilt top. June Inouye used only one piece of fabric for her quilt Abstract View (shown at right).

When creating a more complicated design, cut a few extra windows so that you can "compose" the quilt top. You are now using the motifs in the fabrics, as a painter would compose a picture, selecting and rejecting the components. Cut the windows so any "connecting lines" of the motif will connect when sewn together.

Position the window blocks and reposition as many times as necessary until you are satisfied with the design's composition. Walk away and return to them a few hours or a day later with a fresh perspective. The quilts Road to Hana Bay and Hawaii, Hawaii, on pages 28 and 74, respectively, took Diana a few weeks to compose. At some point, however, you have to tell yourself, "This is enough playing around; it's time to begin sewing this quilt!"

Abstract View, 48" x 60", 1988, by June Inouye. June used a fabric very different from the view she "composed." Notice the complementary, straight line machine quilting in the windows.

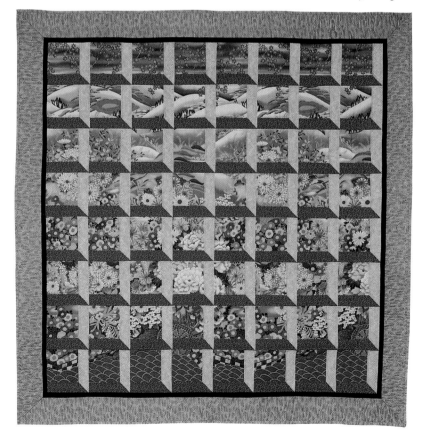

Blue and Gold, 56" x 56", 1999, by Y. S. Lynda Lee. This is only Lynda's second quilt. In a Sampler quilt class (from Diana Leone's book The New Sampler, C&T), Lynda made an Attic Window block. She saw the potential for a whole quilt and spent the following weekend piecing this quilt. She has been spending all of her free time at her sewing machine—she is totally hooked. Her husband thinks she should join Quilter's Anonymous for treatment! Thanks to the new quilters like Lynda for sharing their inspiring quilts in this book.

The Lion and His Lair, 36" x 42", 1999, by Diana Leone. Diana used a large fabric panel from Springs Industries, Inc. for the center focus and a coordinating fabric in the other windows of this project. The center area—the quilt's showcase—was determined and cut, and the blocks around it were cut to "fit." The value of the sashing and its width were determined and the project was assembled. Diana designed the fabrics used in the sashing and border for Northcott/Monarch. The detail at right shows Diana's free motion machine quilting using the plant motifs for inspiration.

Step-by-Step Directions: A Project

The Lion, 36" x 42", 1999, by Cindy Walter.

Throughout the following instructional part of this book, we feature the lion quilt shown here. We used a fabric panel from Springs Industries, and the sashing and border fabrics were designed by Diana Leone for Northcott/Monarch. If you would like to make a similar quilt, here are the fabric requirements:

Lion Quilt Yardage and Cutting Chart

Finished size 36" x 42"

Fabrics	Yardage	Cut
Theme prints	2 yards total	12 - 6" x 8"
Bottom sashing	$^1/_2$ yard	4 - 2$^1/_2$" x 42"
Side sashing	$^1/_2$ yard	4 - 2$^1/_2$" x 42"
Ledge	$^1/_2$ yard	8 - 1" x 42"
Inner border	$^1/_4$ yard	4 - 1$^1/_2$" x 42"
Outer border	1$^1/_4$ yards	4 - 6$^1/_2$" x 43"
Single binding	$^1/_4$ yard	5 - 1$^1/_2$" x 42"
Double binding	$^1/_2$ yard	5 - 2$^3/_4$" x 42"

Use a $^1/_4$" seam for all piecing.

If you are using Perfect Patchwork templates, use them to cut your windows and sashing. Follow the piecing instructions that come with the templates. You will not be using the Fast Ladder sewing method (on page 47).

Theme print

Cut the Window Fabric

Now that you have finished the planning stage, you are ready to cut the windows. Determine the window size, mark the fabric, and cut the windows using rotary equipment. We cut our windows 9" x 6".

Once all of the windows are cut, place them in the correct order on your design wall (or table). If your windows achieve the desired effect, label them before removing them from the design area. Label them A1, A2, B1, B2, etc. by pinning small notes to each window or by writing with a washable pencil in the seam area.

Place four sheets of typing paper around the selected motif to decide the size and picture to cut.

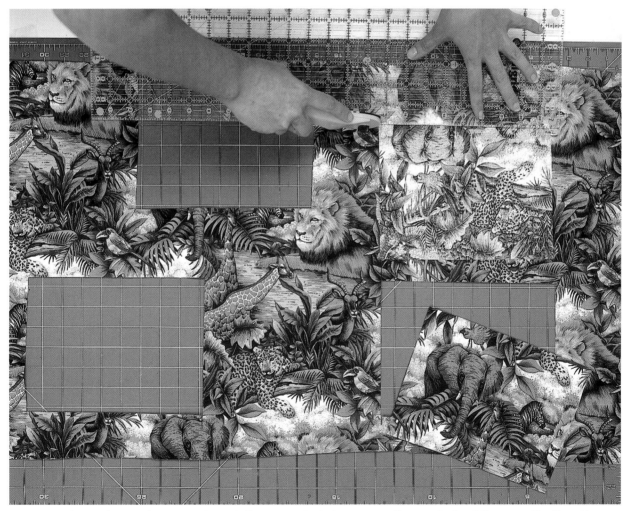

Cutting out the windows with rotary equipment. Place one cut window over another area to "see" the connecting lines, if any.

Cut the Sashing Strips

Use solids or low-contrast prints for the sashing. Cut long strips across the 42″ width. One strip should accommodate four windows, depending on the window's height or width. Calculate the total number of sashing strips you will need. To allow for the miter, remember to **add** the width of the next sashing (plus ¹/₂″ for insurance) to each window measurement. Use a rotary cutter, cutting guide, and cutting mat for fast, accurate cutting. For our quilt, we cut four strips each from both the vertical and horizontal fabrics, at 2¹/₂″ x 42″.

TIP *Diana prefers to cut lengthwise strips because they do not stretch as much as cross-grain strips, which helps keep the quilt squared. To allow for lengthwise cutting, add more fabric to the estimates and plan accordingly. Use the leftovers for the backing or another quilt.*

TIP *Always place your hand on the cutting guide next to the blade, holding your hand up and next to the blade as you cut.*

TIP *Place grip dots on the back of the cutting guide to prevent slippage.*

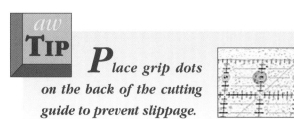

Sew the Quilt Top

Take a little time now to prepare the sewing machine, tools, and sewing area.

Use only high-quality 100-percent cotton thread for machine piecing. Cotton thread has "give" and sews smoothly, while 100-percent polyester thread is too fine and too strong to use on cotton fabrics, causing the seams to pucker and pull. Select a neutral thread color that blends with the fabrics, such as gray or beige.

Use a new size 10, 11, or 12 Jeans (Denim) needle in the sewing machine. Use ¹/₄" seam allowances to make the seam areas less bulky and easier to quilt.

Fill enough bobbins to completely piece the top (three to five).

Place all of the labeled windows in a stack within close reach of the sewing machine. Place a stack of horizontal sashing strips next to the stacked window pieces.

Fast Ladder Sewing

The window pieces are sewn to the long strips of sashing fabric in assembly-line fashion. **A section of sashing is skipped between each window to allow for the area needed to form the miter.** This unsewn space is very important; you must skip **over** this section of the strip. The distance that is skipped, or not sewn, is equal to the width of the second sashing, plus ¹/₂" for cutting insurance (the second sashing is usually the same width as the first sashing). Once cut apart, this unsewn fabric "tail" will be used later to form the miter. The sashing is cut above the edge of each window. The windows are sewn to the second sashing strips, and these strips are cut apart, leaving the tail in the same manner as the first sashing. The 45° miter is sewn and you have a pieced window block. If the sashings are to be sewn to the windows in a different configuration, follow along and then sew yours in the order according to your plan. If the windows get out of order, it is okay because they are labeled and can be reassembled into the planned configuration later.

aw **TIP** *P**lace a length of masking tape on the needle throat plate ¹/₄" from the edge of the needle's right side. The left edge of the tape becomes a sewing guide. This strip of tape is also useful when teaching children or beginners. Mark the strip at ¹/₄" in back of the needle and ¹/₄" in front of it. Use these ¹/₄" seam guides for starting and stopping when sewing the miters. Some feet have a ¹/₄" line marked on the side edge. Use these guides when sewing the miter.*

Sew the First Sashing to the Window

You can sew the side or bottom sashing to the window first. We show sewing the horizontal sashing first:

1 Place one horizontal sashing strip under the presser foot, right side up. Align the right edge of the strip with the right edge of the seam guide (or the presser foot's edge).

2 Pick up the first window piece, R1 (1), and place the bottom edge of the window on top of the long strip, right side down toward the sashing. Match the cut edges one on top of the other. Tip: Move the window fabric two threads to the left, and let the two threads the width of the under strip show. This visual of the extra fabric will ensure that the sashing and window are aligned correctly.

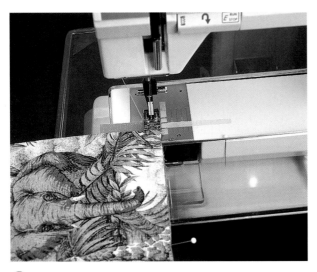

3 Sew, beginning at the top edge of the window.

4 Sew toward the bottom edge until you are **exactly** ¹/₄″ from the bottom edge of the window. Backstitch three or four stitches. It is very important to stop at ¹/₄″ from the edge to leave space for the mitered corner. Some people find it helpful to mark this "¹/₄″ stopping area" with a pencil dot. Hint: If your ¹/₄″ foot has markings in front and behind the needle position, now is the time to use them: stop sewing at the ¹/₄″ mark on the foot. Also, you can use marks on the ¹/₄″ masking tape on the throat plate as a guide to stop ¹/₄″ from the edge (as described on the previous page).

5 Lift the presser foot and pull the fabric back and away from the sewing machine, skipping a section of sashing equal to the width of the sashing, plus ¹/₂″ for cutting room. This unsewn length of fabric, the "tail," will be used later to form the mitered corner. Tip: Pull out extra thread (1″ or so) and replace the fabric under the foot. This will stop the threads from "pulling" the block when you begin to sew.

6 Place the next window block, R1 (2), on top of the sashing. (Remember to leave a length of unsewn sashing between the two windows equal to the width of the sashing, plus ¹/₂″ for cutting room.) Sew from the back edge to exactly ¹/₄″ from the front edge and backstitch, as you did previously.

Sew the Second Sashing to the Window

Using the fast ladder technique, sew all of the window blocks to the second (vertical) sashing strip. This second strip is usually the same width as the first sashing, but depending on your design, it may be a different width.

7 Sew all of the window pieces to the sashing strips in the same manner.

8 Cut the sashing strips apart at the top edge of each window block. Do not "under-cut" the sashing strip; leave the extra fabric tail loose, dangling from the bottom edge of each window.

9 Place a second sashing fabric strip right side up under the presser foot. Place a window block (with the attached first sashing) on top of this long strip, with right sides together (the vertical side of the motif on the underside of the window on top of the sashing). The horizontal sashing will be across the top (do not sew across the horizontal sashing). Align the outside edge of the window on top of the vertical sashing. Let two threads of the sashing show beyond the window fabric so you know it is correctly aligned.

10 Push the first sashing seam allowances up so they are not in the way. Place the needle in the seam of the first sashing and window fabric. Begin right at the seam line ($1/4$" from the edge of the window). Do not sew across the seam allowance. This is important for the miter corner. Sew the seam to the other edge of the window.

Do not cut off the "tail." It will be used to form the 45° miter.

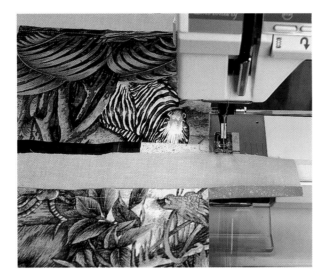

11 Lift the presser foot and pull the window block and sashing strip back and away from the machine. **Do not sew across the first sashing fabric or seam allowance.** This unsewn area of the sashing will be used later for the mitered corner. Cut the threads if they are pulling the fabric.

12 Finish all of the blocks, repeating the previous steps. Sew all of the blocks to the vertical sashing, starting at the horizontal sashing seam line. Remember: If you take a backstitch, do not sew into the seam line; sew forward to the front bottom edge of the window (you do not need to backstitch at this edge, because the next crossing seam will secure the seam end).

13 Cut the sashing fabric apart evenly at the top edge of the sashing and window block. Do not undercut the sashing strip. Leave the extra fabric tail loose, dangling from the bottom edge of each window. Do not cut off the tail, because it will be used for the miter.

Sew the 45° Miter—It's "Sew Easy"!

14 Fold the window on the 45° diagonal, aligning sashing edges, right sides together. The fold is the guideline to align the template and mark the 45° miter onto the sashing fabric. The sashings are the same width; they are now carefully aligned one on top of the other, with right sides together.

15 Place this folded window block on the table in front of you with the sashings toward you.

16 The sashing seam lines will be exactly on top of each other. The outer edges of the sashing should also be perfectly straight, even, and aligned with each other.

17 Push the seam allowances up and toward the window fabric. Pin the sashing seam line together and out of the way of the miter sewing line. Place one pin in the "tails" to hold the two together and aligned and one pin in the sashing seam allowance. Tip: Use Clover Flower head pins; these pins lie flat under the cutting guide and can be ironed.

*N*on-45° *Angles: If the angles of the miter are 45°, you are ready to sew these seams to form the miter, but if the angles of the miter are not 45°, see "Sewing the Non-45° Angle" (page 52).*

18 Place a transparent 45° triangle, or 6″ x 24″ or 6″ x 18″ Omnigrid cutting guide, on top of the window fabric's fold, extending across the sashing at a 45° angle. Mark this line carefully on the sashing with a washable pen or pencil; you will sew this line to create the miter.

19 Pin the marked miter line. The sashing seam allowances should be toward the window block, back and away from the sewing line.

20 Lift the first block carefully and place the miter seam line under the presser foot. Position the needle tip in the exact place where the miter seam will begin. Lower the needle into the sashing fabric exactly where the miter will begin at the window block's corner.

21 Sew from the inside seam line where the sashing and window fabrics meet to the outside edge of the miter, following the marked line. Remove the pin before you sew over it.

22 Open the pieced window block and admire the perfect miter. Trim the mitered seams to ¹/₂″ and trim the loose threads.

23 Sew all of the mitered corners.

24 Press all of the seams away from the window. Press the mitered seam open or toward the bottom sashing. We prefer to press the seams of the miter open whenever possible to avoid bulk.

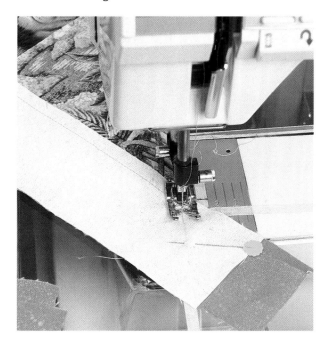

Three or Four Sashings Around the Window

Sewing a Non-45° Angle may appear a little tricky; follow these instructions to make it easy.

- If the sashings are different widths, the miter angle will not be 45°. To determine the angle of the different miters, measure the width and length of one sashing, including the seam allowances. Cut a template to this size. Measure the second sashing size and make a template.
- Place one template exactly on top of the other one, forming an "L."
- Measure ¼" in from the side and bottom corner and ¼" in from the inside edges. Mark dots where these measurements are on the templates.
- Mark a line connecting the dots. Place the bottom template on the top, forming the "L." Trace the line. Make a separate template for each different sashing miter. Use the template to mark the angles on the each sashing.
- Fold the window on the diagonal, with right sides together. Carefully align the marked miter lines on the sashing. The raw edges of the sashings will not align as with a 45° angle.
- Pin, sew, trim, and press.

By the Sea, 21" x 30", 1999, by Diana Leone. Diana machine pieced and quilted this quilt. The center motif is from a Mary Engelbreit fabric (VIP). Diana designed the fabrics used in the crazy quilt block and the sashings (available through Northcott/Monarch). The center crazy quilt block is from Diana's book Crazy With Cotton *(C&T).*

Make the Blocks the Same Size

Once the sashing is sewn to the window blocks you are now ready to trim all of the blocks to the same size. Use a large square gridded cutting guide that is larger than the smallest block (15″ x 15″ or 6″ x 24″).

- The pieced window blocks may vary slightly in size (and probably will). Use Diana's technique to square the blocks and make them the same size.
- Find the smallest block by measuring the width and length of the finished block. One will be smaller than the rest if only by a fraction of an inch. All of the blocks must become the same size.
- Place a gridded cutting guide over the front of this block.
- Align the sashing seam lines to a line on the gridded guide.
- Mark the sashing seam line on the gridded guide with ¹/₄″ wide masking tape. Use the tape line to align to the cut edges of the blocks before trimming them to size. Mark the outer edges of the block on the grid. These lines are the cutting lines to follow when trimming the block's edges.

If you are using a high-quality batting, press the seams open whenever possible. Open seams are easier to machine or hand quilt through and eliminate bulk in the seam areas.

- Place the tape-marked "cutting guide" over the front of a block. Align the marked lines on the template over the seam lines in the block.

- Trim all the edges of each block to the same size.

Sew the Window Blocks Together

Now that you have the window and sashing blocks completed, you are ready to sew them together to create the quilt top. You can do this by sewing the blocks directly to each other or by adding a ledge of fabric in between each block. Either way, you will want to use "matching marks" to make sure the blocks are properly aligned.

Mark "Matching Marks" to Make Perfectly Aligned Blocks

- Using a straightedge, draw a light line on the wrong side of the sashing from the seam line to the edge of the sashing. Mark "match marks" in the sashing seam allowance. These marks will be used to match the seam marked lines of the adjacent blocks when pinning together the seam line to "match mark."
- There will be two marks, one on each side of the sashing, if you have two sashes, three marks if the window block has three sashings, etc. Mark all of the window blocks in this manner. Hint: Diana developed this perfect piecing method of matching the marks. Use this method in the future for all sashing and borders. Matching makes perfect seams and a squared top.
- You are now ready to either add a ledge or sew the window blocks into rows.

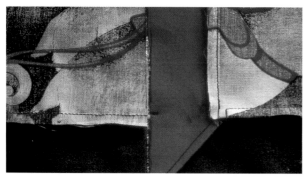

- Press the seams toward the sashing or open as desired.

Sew the Blocks Together Without a Ledge

- Place the labeled quilt blocks on the design wall, right side out, in accordance with your composition. This is the last visual check before sewing. Align the "match marks" on the sashing with the corresponding seam line of the adjacent block.

- Now you are ready to sew the rows together. Align the "match marks" on the sashing edge with the corresponding seam line of the horizontal block (Row 1, Block 1 to Row 2, Block 2, etc.). Pin the rows together and sew, aligning the marked lines on the edge of the sashing to their corresponding seam lines.

- Sew all of the horizontal window blocks together to create rows.
- You have finished the inner top of your first Attic Window. Add the border(s), and the quilt top is completed. If not adding a ledge, skip the next section and go on to "Adding Borders" (on page 56).

The Ledge or Narrow Lattice

Use a ledge or narrow lattice to make the quilt larger and to separate busy blocks. Decide now if you want to add a ledge.

Sew the Rows Together With a Ledge

- Place the labeled quilt blocks on the design wall, right side out, in accordance to your plan. Label the back of each flock (row 1-1, row 1-2).
- Cut the vertical ledge strips to the planned width.

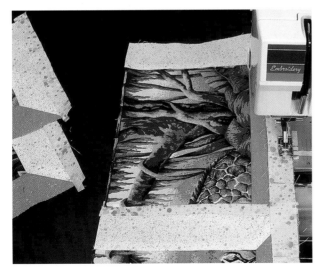

TIP

Cindy recently had problems with pinned-on labels being in the way of her seam lines. She removed the labels and marked the code on each window with a quilter's pen that washes away with the touch of water. Diana labels the blocks by writing in the seam allowance on the back of each block. (She can clearly see the labels on the wrong side of the fabrics as she sews.)

- Place the stack of window blocks next to the machine. Pin a ledge strip to the right-hand side of each block, except the last block in each row. Sew.
- Sew the window blocks to the vertical ledge strips.
- Skip $1/2$" between the blocks to allow for "cutting" room.
- Cut the blocks apart.
- Press the seam to one side or open.
- Mark match marks on the ledge strips.
- Sew the rows together.
- Pin block 1 with its ledge strip to block 2, carefully aligning match marks.
- Continue sewing the adjacent blocks together to form complete rows. Press.
- Cut the horizontal ledge strips to the desired width.
- Mark match marks that correspond with the exact measurements of the seam lines. For example, if the ledge's seam lines are 1", the extended sashing line is 2". These match marks are marked along the edge of the ledge border fabric.
- Pin the seam row 1 to the match marks along the ledge fabric. Sew from end to end.
- Press the seams toward the ledge fabric.
- Sew all of the rows to the ledge fabrics.
- Sew a long ledge strip to the right and left side of the completed inner top. Sew a ledge strip to the top and bottom of the inner top.
- Press all seams toward the ledge fabrics.

Adding Borders

The borders are the quilt's final framework, giving the inner pieced top a finished look. The color of the border will dominate the quilt. Choose a color you wish to feature, or select a color that blends and coordinates with the top. The border can be used to make a small quilt larger. The hand or machine quilting will cause the quilt to become smaller, so make the quilt a few inches larger than the desired finished size. You can trim the edges to the exact size needed before it is bound.

1 Measure the width of the quilt top across its center, then across the top and bottom. The measurements should be the same; note these measurements.

2 Cut these strips the length needed **plus** a distance equal to two border widths. These added measurements will allow the space for the borders' mitered corners.

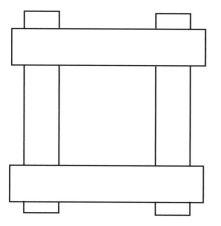

3 Pin a side border to the side of the top (right sides together) from the center out. Remember, you will have extra fabric at the border's ends for the mitered corners.

4 Sew the side border to the quilt top, beginning and stopping ¹/₄″ from the edge of the top. Sew the remaining borders in the same manner.

5 Sew the miter: Fold the quilt top, right sides together, at a 45° angle. Pin the two border fabrics together, carefully aligning the seam lines.

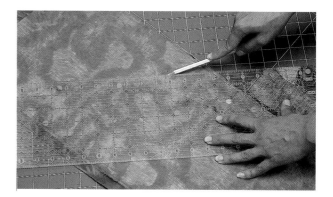

6 Place the ruler exactly at the edge of the quilt top's fold. Extend the ruler over the border fabric.

7 Mark the 45° miter seam line on the border. Pin carefully.

8 Sew the miter, starting exactly at the seam line of the inner top. Sew from the inside seam line to the edge. Trim the excess fabric.

9 Press all of the seams toward the border or open, as desired. Trim the seams and any loose threads.

10 Pat yourself on the back—you have finished your Attic Window top, so step back and admire it!

section 3

Finishing

Planning the Quilting

First, decide how much quilting you want to do. How much time do you have to quilt? Do you want to machine or hand quilt? Do you have a good machine in great working order? Are you willing to buy a walking foot? Can you take a hand or machine quilting class? (We have included a small section in this book on both methods.)

If you would like more details about hand quilting, we refer you to *Fine Hand Quilting*, 2nd Edition, published by Krause Publications, which we co-authored. The book explains all of the new tools of the trade and walks you through the hand quilting technique with detailed color photographs. It also includes a new chapter called "How to Quilt this Quilt" that features traditional and innovative, contemporary hand quilted quilts. There are even a few Attic Window examples in *Fine Hand Quilting*.

For more details about machine quilting, and if you are a beginner in this area, we suggest that you take a class at your local quilt shop, or read one of the many good books written on this topic (see the Bibliography and References section for recommended reading).

Marking the Top

Deciding on the quilting lines is an important step in finishing the quilt. You may wish to quilt free-motion style with a darning foot, following the "theme of the quilt," or stipple in a meandering motion. In this case, you do not have to mark lines on the top.

If you wish to quilt elaborate feathers or other designs from stencils or templates, mark the top after it is ironed and before it is layered with the batting and backing. Marking the quilting lines may take hours or days to successfully complete.

In the course of transferring the quilting design onto the quilt top, you will probably use a variety of marking pencils, depending on the color and the print of the fabrics used in the top. We recommend Berol Verithin pencils or quilter's pencils; use any colors that show enough to see and will wash out. Test the marking tool's lines on scraps of the actual fabrics used in the top, and wash the test piece to make sure the lines wash out.

A variety of marking tools.

If you are using a chalk marker, mark small areas at a time, because the chalk will brush off as you work. The same is true with a disappearing (air-soluble) ink pen; mark only the area you plan to quilt within the hour.

When "echoing" the seam lines, or outlining the edges of the patchwork, try using 1/4" wide masking tape. There is no need to mark the quilting lines because you quilt along the tape's edge. It is definitely easy, fast, and worth a try, especially on dark fabrics where markings may not show. Be careful not to let the quilting needle touch the adhesive side of the tape; the glue will effect the needling. Remove the tape when you are not quilting; it may leave a residue on the quilt's surface.

While tracing or marking with rulers, templates, or stencils, hold your pencil at a 45° angle so it will glide across the fabric smoothly. Make smooth, light strokes that are just dark enough to see. Keep your pencil sharpened because fine lines are easy to follow and will wash out more easily. We have seen many quilts marked with such a heavy hand, that the quilt was ruined (because the markings won't wash out). If you make a mistake while marking, leave it alone and wash it out later. Do not use colored erasers because they have dye in them, usually pink, that will rub into your fabric.

Backing Fabric

It is best to choose the same quality fabric for the back as you used for the top. The color and design of the back should complement and enhance the work involved in making the top. Using only one fabric on the back is beautiful because it will showcase the quilting. We both enjoy making scrap, or pieced backs, from leftover fabrics used in the top. To do this, sew together large pieces of the leftover fabric into any simple design large enough to cover the back.

Preparing the Backing Fabric

A traditional method for selecting the backing fabric is to use a fabric that coordinates with the top. Remember that the quilting stitches will show on the back, so select a thread color that will blend with the backing fabric; the stitches will be hidden on the back. Plan the backing fabric to be two inches larger in all dimensions than the quilt top; the top may slightly shift even though it is securely basted. Bring the extra backing fabric around to the front and pin, or baste, along the edges to protect them from fraying while quilting.

Pre-wash the backing fabric to prevent future shrinkage and to make it easier to quilt. All manufactured fabrics vary in width. Calculate the fabric requirements for the backing based on 42" rather than 44" to allow for any fabric width variation and shrinkage. If your quilt top is more than 42" wide, piece two lengths together, and if your quilt is wider than 84", piece three lengths together. If you need two panels, piece the back with a center panel and two half-side panels; the back will drape better and you will avoid a common problem of a puckered center seam. The backing strips can be placed horizontally or vertically, but vertical seams are best because they aid in the drape of the quilt on the bed or the wall. If you haven't already done so, trim off the selvages before sewing and press the seams to one side or open, if desired. If you are using a good-quality batting, press the seams open to reduce bulk for ease of hand and machine quilting.

Binding Fabric

We suggest using straight-cut binding for straight-edged quilts and bias-cut binding for curved-edged quilts. The binding's width (double- or single-fold) and the quilt's perimeter determine the amount of fabric you will need for the binding. Because an Attic Window quilt usually has straight sides, we've included instructions for either single- or double-fold straight-edged binding. Single- or double-fold binding is a matter of preference; we both use either method, depending on the project. Use double-fold on thicker quilts that may receive more wear and single-fold on thinner wall hangings that may receive little wear.

To determine the amount of fabric needed for straight-edge binding, measure the perimeter of the quilt in inches. Divide this number by 40. This will tell you how many strips to cut cross-grain from your fabric. To find out how much total yardage of fabric you need for the binding, multiply the number of strips by 3" for double binding, or 2" for single binding (these calculations are generous). Cut the binding 2 3/4" wide for double-fold and 1 1/2" wide for single-fold binding.

Batting

Batting is the soft, usually thin, filler that is layered, or sandwiched, between the quilt top and backing. Its function is to add an additional layer to the quilt, providing warmth, a thermal effect, and some loft. It is important to buy the correct type and the best quality batting you can find. When purchasing batting at a quilt shop, ask for the best quality available for the type of quilting you plan to do (hand or machine). The use of quality batting will reward you by being easy to quilt and last the lifetime of your quilt. We recommend premium "bonded and/or treated" batting, which is readily available at your local quilt shop. It is soft, pliable, uniform in thickness, and will not beard or come apart with use. The label will say bonded, premium-quality batting. Inexpensive battings can cause all sorts of disasters, including bearding or fiber migration through the weave of the fabric. Poor-quality unbonded batting can separate and large clumps can form inside the quilt. This unseen layer is so important to your quilts! Make the extra effort to find the best, and you'll be happy in the long run. Quilt shops have researched and carry the best brands available, so seek out a shop in your area, talk to the employees, and rely on their advice.

Batting comes in sheets that are cut to the most common dimensions used for quilts, from crib to king size. It can also be purchased by the yard, in various widths. Batting comes in a variety of thickness (loft), from very thin to thick. Thin-loft batting ($\frac{1}{8}$″ to $\frac{1}{2}$″ thick) gives an old-fashioned flat look and is the easiest to needle (quilt through). Medium-loft batting ($\frac{3}{4}$″ to 1″ thick) is the most commonly used batting and is also easy to needle. Thick-loft batting ($1\frac{1}{4}$″ to 2″ thick) gives you the effect of a comforter and is usually used in quilts or comforters that are tied. (See Diana's book *Crazy With Cotton* to learn how to tie an easy knot that won't come untied.)

Preparing the Batting

There is no need to pre-wash any of the current battings on the market. In the past several years, the major manufacturers have changed how they make batting; not only are they pre-washing the cotton batting for you, but they are also removing the seeds and other natural fibers that used to make it difficult to work with these battings.

Most battings come vacuum-packed in a plastic bag. Take the batting out of the bag and unfold it a day before you intend to baste the quilt. This allows it

TIP *Diana places the batting (out of the bag) in the dryer for a few minutes (on cool-warm), which allows it to relax and fluff. Also, a hair dryer on warm, not hot, held over the flat batting will quickly remove wrinkles.*

Different varieties of batting.

to relax and removes the wrinkles caused by the packaging.

Batting for Machine Quilting

We suggest a thin, high-quality, cotton batting. Cotton batting has a wonderful quality of "holding the layers together" while machine quilting, which is important to help prevent shifting and puckers. It is also thin, drapes well, and is easy to machine quilt.

Batting for Hand Quilting

We suggest a low-loft (fairly thin), bonded, polyester batting. The batting's package should say it is either "bonded" or "treated," which means it has a special kind of coating needed for stability.

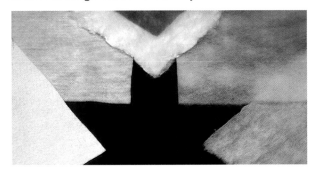

A variety of thin battings.

Layer and Baste the Quilt

Basting holds the quilt's three layers together during the quilting process. Basting is accomplished with one of several different methods. Different tools are used such as thread and needle, safety pins, a basting gun, or spray adhesive for the different techniques.

A quilt sandwich is made up of the top, batting, and backing fabric. You need a large surface, like a table, to position the layers and create the quilt sandwich. Raise the table with 4" x 4" blocks placed under the legs to make the working surface high enough to be comfortable. As a last resort, if you don't have a large table, you can use a tile (not carpeted) floor (this will be hard on your body, but it works). If you plan to use a quilt spray adhesive as your method of basting, spray the "glue" between each layer as you follow these steps. Layering a quilt on a table is really a two-person job, so ask a friend to help.

- Raise the table's height by putting books or blocks under each leg until it is at a comfortable height.
- Find the centerlines of the table and backing fabric.
- Lay the backing fabric right side down on the table, matching centerlines. Tape the backing fabric to the table with masking tape, if desired.
- Center the batting over the backing fabric; carefully smooth any wrinkles.
- Tape the center of the backing's edges to the center of the table's edges.
- Center the quilt top right side up on the batting. Carefully smooth away wrinkles, working from the center outward, being careful not to stretch the quilt top out of shape.

Thread Basting

This is a traditional method of basting and that most often used in hand quilting. You will need:

Large table (36" x 72" is perfect)
Two assorted sized packages of Milliners needles, sizes 4, 5, or 6
White cotton thread
Thimble
Scissors
Books or wooden blocks to raise the table height
Top, layered with backing and batting

- Raise the table's height by placing books or wooden blocks under each leg until its height is comfortable.
- Thread about a dozen Milliner needles (size 4-6) with long double strands of white thread.
- Cut the thread long enough to reach from the center of the quilt to its edges and back again.
- Tie a large "waste knot," or roll knot, in the end of the thread. (The knot is called a waste knot because it will be cut off, or wasted.) Never use this knot for quilting or sewing. The large knot is easy to clip away when ready to remove the basting thread.
- Start in the center of the quilt, making two or three 2" long stitches, and then pull the length of the thread through the quilt. Baste vertically and horizontally about 3" apart, always from the center out.

- When you reach the part of the quilt that is hanging over the edge of the table, leave the threaded needle in the quilt's edge. Once the entire surface on the table is basted, pull the quilt to one side, moving the unbasted area onto the table. Baste the remaining areas.
- Check to make certain there are no wrinkles on the back. If so, clip the basting threads in that area and rebaste.

Safety-pin Basting

Cindy prefers safety pin basting and has used this technique on small and large quilts for years.

- Use nickel or brass-plated pins, size 0 or 1, depending on the batting's thickness (the thinner the batting, the smaller the pin).
- Begin in the center and work your way out to the edges. Slide a safety pin into the top, batting, and backing, and then back up through all of the layers (without closing it) every 3″ to 4″.
- Once all of the pins are in, go back and close them.

Fabric Spray Adhesives

We have used two different fabric spray adhesives, KK 2000 and 505, to baste our quilts. We found the sprays to be fast and efficient when working with small quilts. The sprays temporarily hold the quilt layers together and do not effect the needling. We do not recommend using any chemicals on heirloom-quality quilts. The spray is applied to one side of the batting, and the top is placed on top of the batting. The spray is applied to the other side of the batting and placed over the wrong side of the backing.

Basting or "Tagging" Gun

This is one of Diana's tools of choice. It is a plastic gun with a thin needle on the end that shoots a plastic anchoring string (tag) through all of the layers and back to the top. Look for a quality brand with a thin needle. Diana prefers the Dennisons Fine Fabric Plus brand because it is the only one she has found with a thin needle. Other brands are inadequate for quilt basting and should not be used. We don't recommend the basting gun for heirloom-quality quilts because the needle may leave small holes that will show up on some fabrics. Use old scissors when it is time to remove the tags. A great advantage of the "tagger" gun is you can machine quilt right over the tags and remove them after you finish quilting.

The trick of using a tagging gun is to push the plastic tag through the front to the back and out the front. The tag is very secure and holds the three layers together.

Hand Quilting

The quilting is the reward of the piece-maker. Some of you may have read *Fine Hand Quilting*, our book on the subject. We highly recommend doing this if you are a new quilter, because we are not able to go into everything that is explained in that book here. If you have read the book or are an experienced hand quilter, you are ready to quilt.

American Folk Art, 31" x 31", 1987, hand quilting by Sondra Rudey. One single fabric was used to compose the window scene.

Left: Christmas Joy, 23" x 42", 1999, by Marian Lorenzen. Marian used Marti Michell perfect Patchwork Templates to quickly and perfectly cut the pieces for the top. The Christmas ornament designs are from "Here Comes Santa" designs by Nancy Halvasen, Art to Heart. Marian embroidered the ornament designs by hand with a long quilting stitch. Her hand quilting stitches on the border are beautiful, uniform, and short.

The goal of hand quilting is to make uniformly short, straight, and even stitches that hold the quilt layers together. You may take one stitch at a time or form several on the needle at once. To become skillful, you will need to learn to use some important tools, including a thimble, 100-percent cotton quilting thread, a hoop, and a very short quilting needle (10, 11, or 12 between).

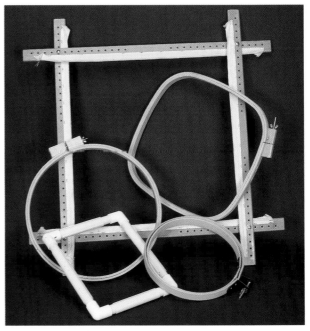

A variety of hand quilting hoops.

The Hand Quilting Process

- Place the center of the basted quilt in a 14", or larger, hoop. Place a thimble on the longest finger of your writing hand; it will push the needle through the quilt's layers.
- Use an 18" length of thread. Tie a single knot near the end that was cut off the spool. Insert the needle between the layers $1/2$" before where you want to begin the quilting line. Bring the needle up at the starting point and pop the knot so it sinks into the batting.
- Insert the needle through the top where you want to start quilting. Push it through the layers until the tip of the middle or forefinger of the under hand receives it. Keeping pressure on the tip of the needle will help it push back up through the top.

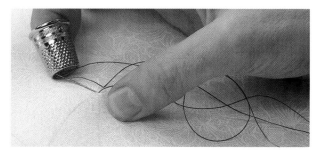

- With the thimble holding the eye-end of the needle, lay the eye end of the needle downward and firmly push the tip of the needle back up through the back and up to the quilt's top. The thumb on the quilting hand is important; it must push the fabric down and out of the way so the needle can come back up. Continue this up and down, rocking motion, forming several stitches at a time on the needle.

- To end, tie a knot close to the quilt. Take a tiny stitch, bringing the needle up $1/2$" away and "popping" the knot between the layers.

Please refer to Diana Leone and Cindy Walter's new book **Fine Hand Quilting** *for thorough hand quilting instructions.*

Machine Quilting

Machine quilting is a fast and efficient way to finish your Attic Window quilt. Analyze the project to determine where you will place the quilting stitches. Your sewing machine must be clean and in good working order, and you must have a large working surface. If you cannot lower the sewing machine so it is even with its cabinet, purchase an extension table. You must use a good quality thread. We suggest machine quilting (not hand quilting) thread in the bobbin and on top. As you become more experienced, try all of the different decorative threads available. For straight-line quilting, use a walking foot on your sewing machine so the quilt layers will feed evenly through the machine. For free-motion quilting, such as stippling, use a darning foot.

We recommend practicing machine quilting stitches on a "sample sandwich." To make a sample sandwich, cut a 14" square from two pieces of fabric and one piece of cotton batting. Lightly baste the layers

Purple Sky, 30" x 36", 1999, by Dorothy Draper Jacques, quilted by Cindy Walter. "Coming from a long line of quilters, it somehow skipped my generation. But, inspired by my daughter, Cindy Walter, I pieced this wall hanging together in two days. I wanted the quilt to simulate 'dusk,' with just a few birds in the sky. Cindy machine quilted it for me and now I am hooked on patchwork." This quilt showcases a very simple machine quilted stipple stitch.

together with your preferred basting method. Practice quilting straight lines with a walking foot, and then put a darning foot on the sewing machine and practice free-motion quilting.

For machine quilting you only need a few supplies:
- Sewing machine
- Walking foot (required)
- Free-motion darning foot (optional)
- Topstitch or denim needle, size 80 or 90
- Cotton machine quilting thread (for bobbin and top)
- Quilter's gloves or machine quilting hoop (both optional)

Straight Line Quilting

Straight-line quilting is used for quilting in the ditch of seams, echoing around patchwork, or to crosshatch (grid) the entire quilt.
- Set the machine to normal straight sewing. Use cotton quilting thread in the bobbin and on top and a larger needle, such as a darning or topstitch.

- Quilt the long seam lines (in the ditch) between the blocks, working from the center of the quilt out to the edges. Quilt both the horizontal and vertical seams. Then, quilt the seam lines of the sashing and other patchwork areas in the blocks.
- Quilt enough to hold the quilt top, batting, and backing securely together and to the specifications of the batting packaging. Some cotton battings require a minimum of quilting every 3″, while others only need to be quilted every 10″.

Habitat, 30″ x 37″, 1999, by Diana Leone. The "Habitat 1" fabric designed by Jane Kriss for Northcott/Monarch inspired Diana to make this quilt. Rain and Mist fabrics, designed by Diana for Northcott/Monarch, were used in the sashings and borders.

- Use a walking foot on the machine.

Detail of Cindy Walter's Snippet Garden; this quilt was free-motion quilted (see page 5 for full quilt).

Free-motion Quilting

We both enjoy the liberty of free-motion quilting; we are artists painting with our thread and needle onto the canvas, the quilt. It is easy, once you get the hang of it, and "mistakes" don't show. Use free-motion quilting to quilt designs on the quilt or simply stipple the entire surface.

Once you are comfortable with the correct rhythm, you can create all types of stitches such as stipples, meanderings, squiggles, or zigzags, or you can simply follow the designs of the printed fabric. Always start in the middle of the quilt and rotate out toward the edges. Do not skip over areas to leave for later, because you will end up with puckers on the back. Work slowly and do not stretch the quilt out of shape. Try quilter's gloves because they allow you to move the quilt easily, and you can feel if there is a pucker, or other trouble, forming on the back.

- Set the machine to normal straight sewing. Use cotton quilting thread in the bobbin and on top and a larger needle, such as a darning or topstitch.
- Put the darning foot on the machine and drop the feed dogs.

- You will be quilting in all directions, without turning the quilt, by guiding it with your hands. The stitch length will be determined by how fast you move your hands and how fast the machine is running. Beginners have a tendency to run the machine too slowly and move their hands too quickly. The secret is to run the machine semi-fast (75-percent of maximum speed) and move your hands semi-slowly at a steady pace. Learn the correct rhythm and your stitches will be consistent and an even length.
- Quilt enough to hold the quilt top, batting, and backing securely together and to the specifications of the batting packaging. Some cotton battings require a minimum of quilting every 3″, while others only need to be quilted every 10″.
- Try decorative threads once you are comfortable.

The Attic Window is a great quilt for practicing machine quilting. Select a good quality cotton thread to practice. When you have gained some confidence, try one of the many specialty threads available.

Binding

The binding is the fabric sewn to the outer edges of the quilt to encase and finish the edge. The fabric should be of the same quality as was used on the quilt's front and back. You can use the same colored fabric as the quilt's outer border, chose a contrasting fabric, or the binding can also be pieced, using multiple colorful fabrics. If you do the latter, the eye will follow the active colors and bring the focus back to the center of the quilt. The binding serves as the final frame around your quilt.

When quilts have curved edges, cut the binding fabric from the fabric's bias (45° angle) and piece these strips together. A bias binding will ease and stretch around curved edges such as a Double Wedding Ring quilt. We have not included continuous bias cutting directions, because this method isn't used often today. (See *The New Sampler Quilt* for thorough bias binding instructions.)

When quilts have straight sides, bindings are cut on the straight of the grain (lengthwise preferred if you have enough fabric) to make the edges of the quilt as straight and squared as possible. A single-fold binding is used on wall quilts, thin quilts, and those receiving little wear, whereas double-fold binding is used on large bed quilts and those receiving more wear.

Make the binding strip by cutting parallel strips of fabric (1¹/₂″ for single, 2³/₄″ for double) with scissors or rotary cutting equipment. Piece the strips together into one long, continuous strip. The length should match the project's perimeter, plus a little extra. For example, a double-sized quilt is 90″ by 108″. You will need a binding that is 396″, plus about 12 inches extra, or about eleven strips of 40″ wide fabric. For double binding, fold it in half, right sides out, and press.

For photography reasons, the pictures show stitching without a walking foot. We both recommend the use of a walking foot (dual feed foot) to sew the binding to the quilt's edge.

Double-fold Straight Cut Binding

1 Align the raw edges of the binding with the front side edge of the quilt, beginning about 10″ from a corner. Fold the end at a 45° angle. Insert a few pins at the beginning of the binding to hold it in place. Do not pin the binding to all of the quilt's edges. You may need to "ease" along the binding as you sew.

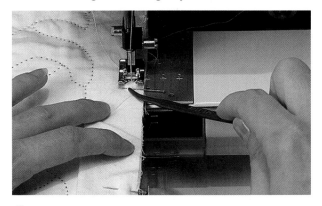

2 Begin sewing 3″ down from the folded end. Sew ¹/₄″ in from the raw edges.

3 Stop stitching ¹/₄″ from the corner. Backstitch. Lift the needle out of the fabric (this is important). Pull the quilt a few inches away from the needle to loosen the threads. Turn the quilt one quarter counter-clockwise. Fold the binding straight up (forming a 45° angle).

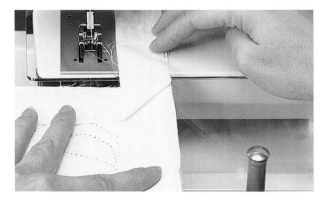

4 Fold the binding in front and down over the angle. The top folded edge must be even with the top edge of the quilt. Beginning at the top edge, continue sewing. Sew all of the quilt's edges. Repeat the miter step at the corners.

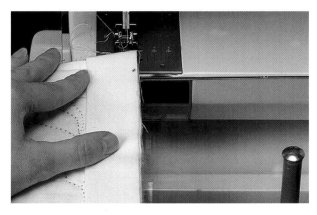

5 To finish the binding end, place the unsewn end over the beginning (folded end) of the binding. Cut the end 1/2″ longer than the beginning edge and insert the unsewn, cut end into the folded edge of the binding. For single-fold binding, simply place the end over the folded beginning edge. Pin and sew the seam across the overlapped ends to finish the seam.

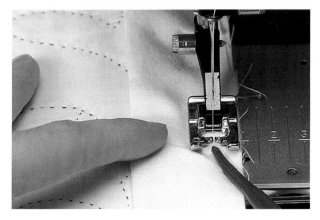

A Purple Thang is used to hold down the binding as it is fed under the foot.

6 Bring the folded edge of the binding around to the back of the quilt.

7 Tuck in the corner, forming a mitered corner of the front and back.

8 Hand-stitch the folded edge to the quilt back using a blind hemstitch.

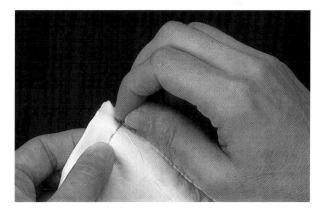

The Finishing Touches

Labeling the Quilt

It is important for you to document your work. One easy way to do this is to make a label. Write your name, address, and any important information on this piece of fabric with a waterproof pen and hand sew the label to the back of the quilt. There are also decorative pre-made labels available at your local quilt shop.

Book cover label. Diana color copied the cover of Fine Hand Quilting onto treated fabric by June Taylor.

Hanging the Quilt

Sew a sleeve, rod pocket, or casing to the quilt's top back edge. Cut the strip 9″ wide from the same fabric as the backing fabric (if possible). Piece the strips if needed so the sleeve equals the exact width of the quilt's top edge. Hand sew it to the quilt about ¹/₂″ from the top back edge. Slip a thin (¹/₄″ x 1¹/₂″) board through the sleeve, allowing ¹/₄″ or more to show on each end. Nail the board to the wall on each end with a short, thin nail. If you are using a round dowel to hand the quilt, pinch a ¹/₂″ fold of extra fabric along the outer side of the sleeve before sewing it to the quilt. The fold will absorb the dowel's roundness, and there will not be a bulge across the front of the quilt.

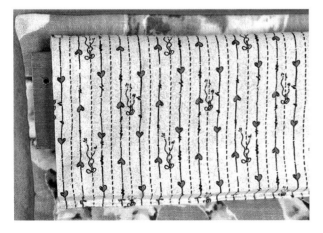

Cleaning the Quilt

A quilt, depending on its use, may need to be washed during its lifetime. If the quilt is stable and the fabric was prewashed, you will be able to hand or carefully machine-wash it; dry cleaning is not recommended. If the quilt is hanging on the wall, it can be lightly vacuumed to remove dust.

When washing a quilt, use a phosphorus-free soap, because detergents have harsh chemicals that may destroy the quilt. We recommend the purest soap available, called Orvus. Use one or two capfuls in a washing machine set on a gentle cycle. Lightly spin the quilt to remove excess water and place the quilt and a large towel in the dryer for 10 to 20 minutes. Remove the quilt before it is completely dry, straighten it on a large sheet on the floor, and allow it to finish drying.

For a delicate or old quilt, hand wash it by using one or two capfuls of Orvus soap (or any other phosphorus-free soap) in a bathtub full of warm water. Gently place the quilt in the water and push it up and down until it is completely wet. Let it soak for 20 minutes (for a dirty quilt, you may have to repeat this process). Drain the bathtub and refill with clean water. Gently push the quilt up and down to rinse. Drain the bathtub and slightly squeeze the excess water from the quilt. Repeat this process until the water runs clear of soap. Dry the quilt outside on a warm day, away from direct sunlight. If drying on the ground, lay a clean sheet over a plastic sheet, and then position the quilt on top of the sheet. Check the quilt every hour or so, turning it until it is dry. If you have a clean clothesline out of the sun, use it, hanging the quilt over two lines.

Storing the Quilt

The best way to store a quilt is to lay it out flat on an unused bed. It the quilt is to be stored in a closet or cedar chest, place a large, clean sheet on the floor, fold the sheet and the quilt together, and place in the storage area. Unfold the quilt at least once a year and refold in a different area to prevent wear on the fold lines. If you have room, a tube about 6 inches in diameter and the width of the quilt is a perfect storage tool. Place the quilt on a sheet and roll the two around the tube. Never store a quilt in a sealed plastic bag. Take your quilts out of storage and enjoy them whenever possible.

Gallery of Attic Window Quilts

Traditional, Innovative, and Special Themes

Looking Through the Windows of Your Life, 97¹/₂" x 108", 1993, by Jean Soderstrom. Family and friends made the window blocks for Jean's late husband, Bill, for his seventy-fifth birthday. The quilt, which documents Bill's life, was given to him at a surprise birthday party. He was overwhelmed and cried with joy upon receiving it.

"While in a shop he said, 'You haven't seen anything until you see the quilt my wife made for me.' Then he went to the car and took it into the store to show off. He would be so proud to have his quilt in the Attic Windows book. He went home to be with The Lord two days before Diana and Cindy's letter arrived expressing interest in publishing the quilt. I have a feeling that he is looking down on us with great pride. Thank you for this honor of sharing what has now become a memorial of Bill's life with the world. I encourage everyone to document his or her family's life in an Attic Window quilt."

Spring at Shinn Pond, 37" x 45", 1999, by Susan Marcia Arrow. Susan enjoys the scenery around the pond as she takes her early morning bike rides and was inspired to make this quilt. Finding the perfect fabrics was the challenge. She "composed" the scene using a variety of fabrics from many manufacturers. Susan began making quilts only eight months ago! She enjoys the search for mood-setting fabrics and plans to make many more quilts.

Kitties in the Window, 38" x 52", 1999, by Karen Arzamendi. Karen cut out the kitty motifs from a fabric panel, then appliquéd them onto a light blue background. (Diana Leone designed all of the fabrics, except the kitten fabric.)

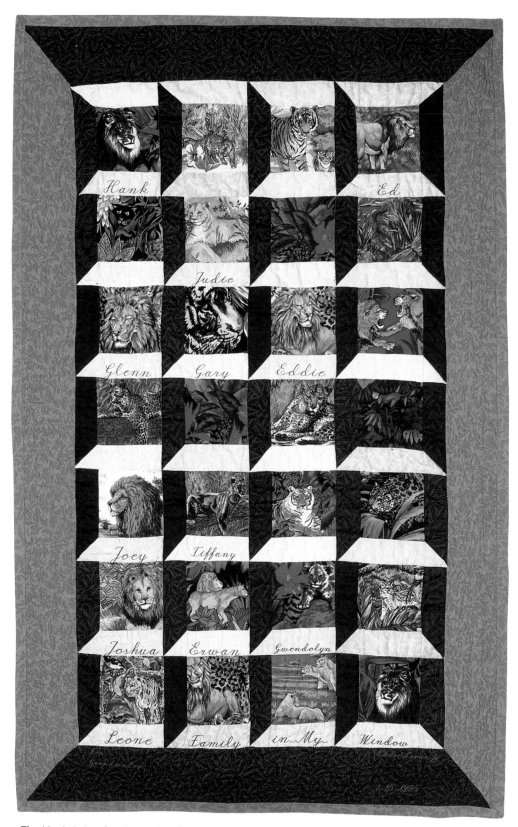

The Lion's Lair—Our Leone Family, 40" x 52", 1990, by Eddie Leone. Eddie made this quilt for his grandmother, Lucille Leone, for her eightieth birthday. Each of the windows represents a different family member; each person's name is freeform machine embroidered in the sashing. A theme quilt is a great reason to collect your favorite fabrics. The Attic Window provides a perfect format to showcase many fabrics. This quilt uses 28 different lion fabrics.

Neptune's Window II, 13" x 13", 1999, by Shelba Jensen. This hand-quilted miniature quilt features a look into an aquarium. The bright-colored sashing and ledge create a wonderful illusion of depth.

Gifts of Nature, 29¹/₂" x 35¹/₂", 1998, by Olga Bratkovskaia. Olga was inspired to make this quilt for her dining room by the fabric's wonderful colors and print.

Hawaii, Hawaii, Every Room Has an Ocean View, 96" x 80", 1988, by Diana Leone. Diana made this quilt as a tribute to her mother who lived in Hawaii in the 1920s. She used to tell Diana about this exciting time in her life—a carefree, happy time of the flapper, cruises, and evening swims in the warm surf. The challenge for this quilt was collecting the unique fabrics; Diana wanted to use different fabrics in each window. The quilt has 42 windows with 37 different fabrics, which she collected from shops around the world.

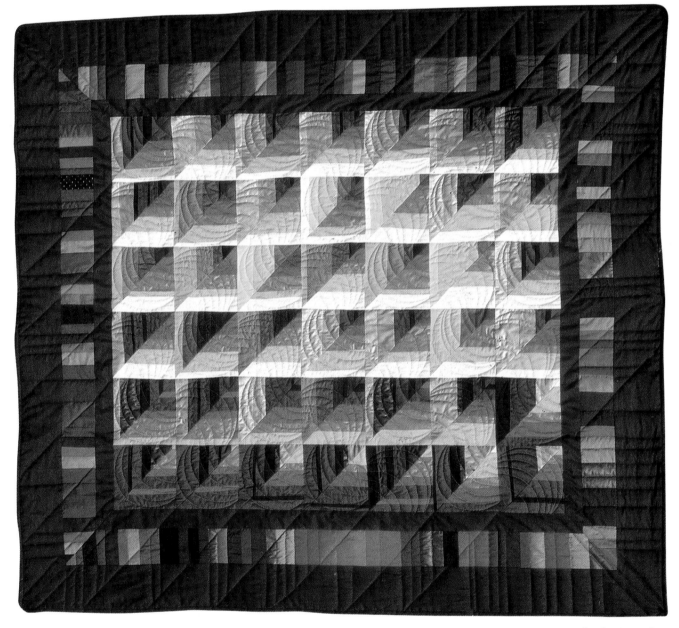

Private Places, 58" x 65", 1983, by Margaret Miller. This beautiful, colorful quilt, from one of Margaret's innovative books, Strips that Sizzle (That Patchwork Place.), is similar to an Attic Window quilt.

Bricks and Boards, 30" x 36", 1986, by Mary Ellen Hopkins. Scrap fabrics were used for this quilt. Notice the different sized windows and the innovative way the sashings appear to be part of the border.

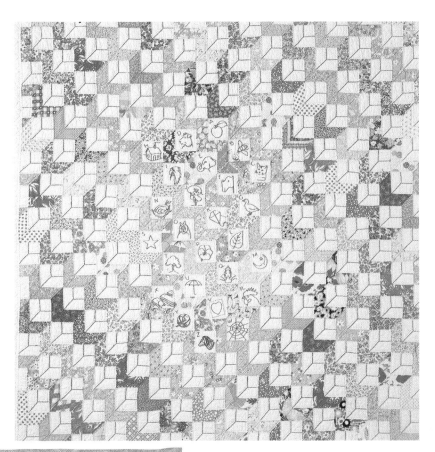

52" x 70", 1930s. This quilt is a pieced and embroidered variation of the Attic Window using more than 100 different fabrics. The alphabet and motifs are embroidered in the center area. Collection of Diana Leone.

Window Box, 42" x 38", 1998, by Kelly Simbirdi. After Kelly made four window blocks, each with a four-grid window, she added the 2" sashes and the $^1/_2$" ledge strips to three sides. Finally, the wide bottom window boxes were pieced, and the flowers were fused using Steam-A-Seam2. This creative and effective Attic Window quilt is one you can make, too!

The Wonder Beyond the Window, 44" x 44", 1999, by Barbara Malanowski-Casty. Barbara, who lives in the tiny village of Scharans, Switzerland, was inspired to use hand-dyed fabrics from Monika Speyer of Augsburg, Germany. Barbara's secret for the blocks is the 1:3 proportion ($^3/_8$" to 1$^1/_8$" are in the smallest block, 1$^1/_2$" to 4$^1/_2$" in the next, and 6" to 18" in the largest). The "Golden Mean" proportions work in quilts as in all art. Notice how the sashings variegate in color.

Who Needs PMS to Eat Chocolate? 38" x 52", 1998, by Debbie Sylvester. Debbie was inspired to make this quilt by a pregnant friend who loved chocolate. The quilt is a chocolate bar comprised of 14 brown Attic Window blocks set on-point with a white background. The bite and crumbs were made using Cindy's Snippet Sensations technique. Debbie used silver lamé for the wrapper—great idea!

School Days Patchworkappliqué, 28" x 18", 1999, by Diana Leone. This single window, which showcases a special printed fabric from Thimbleberries, Inc., was hand appliquéd and machine quilted by Diana. She developed this unique hand appliqué technique in 1985. The figures appear to be walking out of the window and onto the sashing below the picture. This innovative technique is easy and adds a new dimension to a piece.

Patchworkappliqué™ Diana Leone 1985. See Hawaii, Hawaii on page 74 for more examples of Patchworkappliqué.

The raw edges of the appliqué brought through the open seam line. The feet will be hand appliquéd.

The feet are hand appliquéd. Free-motion quilting finishes the quilt.

Through My Garden Window, 46" x 30", 1999, by Karen Arzamendi. This is the view from the inside looking out at a flower garden. Karen appliquéd a bird perched on an overhanging tree branch. This quilt, made of fabrics by Diana Leone for Northcott/Monarch, is embellished with buttons and silk ribbon embroidery.

Hawaiian Garden, 70" x 82", 1999, by Cindy Walter. Cindy lived in Hawaii for nine years; the flowers of the islands are very dear to her heart. The windows and borders are from Hawaiian fabric, which she purchased on the islands in 1998. The red and gold fabrics are by Diana Leone tor Northcott/Monarch. This quilt top will provide a fun format to free motion machine quilt.

Humphry and Friends, 60" x 60", 1995, by Kelly Simbirdi. The windows are Crazy with Cotton blocks, featured in Diana Leone's Crazy with Cotton *(C&T). The use of primary colors in the sashing adds to the three-dimensional effect; it appears like the viewer is in a submarine, looking out the windows. This is a great theme quilt for a child's room. Notice the use of the wide sashing and narrow ledge. The use of the ledge helps balance and showcase the busy strips-pieced windows.*

View from a California Attic, 46" x 34", 1999, by Virginia Schnalle. One large window showcases a painted California foothills scene. The quilt features a thread-painted, appliquéd tree in the foreground and machine-appliquéd and -fused (using Steam-a-seam2) vase and flowers sit on the windowsill. Virginia used Touch of Gold fusible interfacing to stabilize the window fabric while thread painting. Notice the elaborate quilting pattern in the border.

Attic Window, 42" x 42", 1999, by Jan Thompson. Jan was inspired by Diana's 1999 fabric line "Flowers from My Gardens, Hibiscus" for Northcott/Monarch. The Attic Window was made to look as though the viewer is looking out of the house and into the garden. The flower motifs were "fussy cut" around the edges and fused in place with Steam-a-seam2. This is a great solution for a fast and easy project.

John, Jan's 6-year-old son, is a very visual little man. He and his mom love to look at the hues and tints of the sky in the morning and evening. Nothing works better at calming him down when he is excited than to find a range of color for him to gaze upon. according to Jan, he was so excited when he saw the background fabric, "Earth, Sea, and Sky," for this quilt (designed by Diana for Northcott/Monarch): "We were gazing upon the morning sky one very chilly winter morning, and could not define in acceptable English, a few wonderful hues across the mountains as the sun was rising. We came up with 'pinkallow' and 'orple.' The clouds in this quilt are 'pinkallow!' John made me promise that I would try to educate people as to the existence of our new names for these magnificent colors and I try never to break a promise." Diana is going to count on John's expertise in naming the colors in her next fabric line!

Springtime Paradise, 1999, Virginia Rojas. Virginia created this quilt for her office wall; now she can sit with a cup of tea and look out her window to her favorite flower garden. She pieced the background using Diana Leone's Crazy with Cotton method and created the flowers using Cindy Walter's Snippet Sensation technique. Notice the one-point perspective from the center emphasizes the depth in the window.

She Loved the Trees, 55" x 65", 1999, by Myra Mitchell. Myra made this quilt in memory of her grandmother, Minnie, who loved the trees and flowers in anyone's garden. Myra's design ideas came from the lighting in the evening, when the moon is shining on the trees and bushes, reflecting teal, black, and purple through black and purple windowsills. The use of the dark teal print and the dark sashing sets the mood and provides a somber reminder of the places Minnie loved.

Dogs in the Attic, 18" x 18", 1999, by Marian Lorenzen. Marian used Marti Michell's Perfect Patchwork templates to accurately cut the pieces for this top. Her piecing and quilting skills are apparent in her little quilt.

Halloween Quilt, 29" x 42", 1999, by Kelly Simbirdi. This innovative quilt required a lot of planning. The windows and sashings are curved and could not be fast-pieced. To create the curved blocks, Kelly had to draw the design on paper and make actual templates. She cut out several of the motifs from the theme fabric and hand appliquéd them to the quilt. The characters seem to be literally jumping out of the quilt!

Birth of a Star, 35" x 41", 2000, by Jan Phelps. Jan took an Attic Window class with instructor Olga Bratkovskaia, who is known for having a good eye for color. Jan is on a journey to learn about color; she has a difficult time using lights. The white fabric was a gift from Nancy, a fellow guild member. When Jan hung the colored fabrics on a design board, it looked like a Giant Nebula, where stars are born.

African Experience, 41" x 48", 2000, by Rosaland Hannibal. For this Attic Window quilt, Rosaland used her favorite photographs from her first trip to Nairobi and Zimbabwe. She feels the large photo in the center of the quilt is the best one she has ever taken; it is a stop on a walking tour of Victoria Falls. Rosaland used Photo Effects photo transfer paper by Transfer Magic to transfer the photos onto cloth. Because all of the photos were of the outdoors, she chose fabrics that symbolized nature as in the green and sky blue sashings. The border fabric added a "lush" feeling. The windows are 10" x 16" (center), 4" x 4" (top and bottom), and 5" x 7" (along the sides), the sashing is 1¹/₂" wide, the lattice is 1" wide, and the border is 7" wide.

Children-themed Quilts

Toys Are Us, 28" x 35", by Gwen Woodard. Gwen, from the Kenai Fabric Center in Kenai, Alaska, machine pieced, embroidered, and machine quilted this quilt. The embroidery appliqués are from the Crown Collection I, and the script is the "Kids" font, both done on a Husqvarna/Viking Designer embroidery machine.

Crayola Counting Book, 52" x 44", 1999, by Vivian Rodriguez, machine quilted by Melodee Wade. This quilt was made using a coloring book fabric panel. Primary colors used in it would attract any child learning how to count. The sashing colors were coordinated with the primary colors used in the panel fabrics. Vivian, who has made many children's quilts, found the Attic Window to be a perfect pattern to showcase the panel fabrics she loves to use.

Attic Toys, 32" x 40", 1999, by Cindy Walter. Cindy divided this charming Spring's panel into six pieces. She wanted to separate the finished window blocks with a ledge. The printed green fabric helped keep the sashings more neutral and not clash with the theme print. The motifs are free-motioned quilted. The four outer windows are 10" x 9", the two inner windows are 10" x 7", the sashing is 1½", and the ledge is ½".

The Family Pets, 24" x 24", 1999, by Nancy Montique, machine quilted by Cindy Walter. Nancy made this quilt in a workshop with Cindy Walter. Nancy's experience as a seamstress came in handy; her piecing is perfect.

Clay's Quilt, 34" x 42", 1999, by Dianne Chipman. Dianne and her sister, Katherine Duncan, share a passion for quilting and made identical quilts for upcoming grandchildren. This quilt was made for her most recent grandson. Dianne created the window motifs by using Bernina's Suzy's Zoo Embroidery patterns. Used with permission, Suzy's Zoo, San Diego, CA.

A Year in a Bear's Life, 62$^{1}/_{2}$" x 88", 1999, by Cecile Jaffrennou and June Jones. This wonderful quilt is a perfect use of the Attic Window pattern. June and Cecile used the instructions in Diana's original Attic Windows book to make this quilt. Luckily, they came to Diana to have this quilt appraised. She saw it and asked them to share it with you here.

The quilt was made for Cecile's daughter, who is also June's goddaughter. This twin-sized quilt uses a large selection of brightly-colored novelty bear motif fabrics that depict the months of the year. The months, seasons, and holidays are featured in each window. It was hand and machine appliquéd with hand embroidery accents. Reverse appliqué was used to create the central "Big Bear" in the two large windows, to make it appear that her left arm is on top of the yellow horizontal sashing. A special border fabric, adorned with honeybees, keeps all of the bears in the quilt very happy.

An example of the thoughtful detail in each window of this quilt.

Monterey, 36" x 44", 1999, by Olga Bratkovskaia. Olga made this quilt, her first, for her daughter Natalia.

Bibliography and References

Better Homes and Garden's America's Heritage Quilts. Des Moines, IA: Meredith Corp.

Shackelford, Anita. *Appliqué with Folded Cutwork.* Paducah, KY: American Quilter's Society. 1999.

Leone, Diana. *Crazy with Cotton.* Lafayette, CA: C&T. 1996.

Squire, Helen. *Create with Helen Squire: Hand and Machine Quilting.* Paducah, KY: American Quilter's Society. 1999.

Noble, Maurine. *Decorative Threads.* Bothel, WA: That Patchwork Place. 1998.

Leone, Diana and Cindy Walter. *Fine Hand Quilting,* 2nd Ed. Iola, WI: Krause Publications. 2000.

Hargrave, Harriet. *Heirloom Machine Quilting.* Lafayette, CA: C&T. 1995.

Noble, Maurine. *Machine Quilting Made Easy.* Bothel, WA: That Patchwork Place. 1994.

Fons, Marianne and Liz Porter. *Quilter's Complete Guide.* Birmingham, AL: Oxmoor House. 1993.

QUILTER'S Newsletter magazine. Leman Publications, Inc.

Bonsib, Sandy. *Quilting Your Memories.* Bothel, WA: Martingale & Company. 1999.

McClun, Diana and Laura Nownes. *Quilts!, Quilts!!, Quilts!!!* Lincolnwood, IL: Quilt Digest. 1997.

Sears, Roebuck and Co. *Century of Progress in Quilt Making.* 1937.

Walter, Cindy. *Snippet Sensations.* Iola, WI: Krause Publications. 1996.

Brandon, Reiko M. *The Hawaiian Quilt.* Honolulu, HI: Booklines Hawaii, Ltd. 1993.

Leone, Diana. *The New Sampler Quilt.* Lafayette, CA: C&T. 1996.

Sources and Suppliers

For seminars or lectures contact:
Diana Leone
21700 Caleara Creek Court
San Jose, CA 95120
dianaleone@hotmail.com
www.Dianaleone.com
Seminars, lectures, studio tours, antique and new quilts
   for sale.

Cindy Walter
c/o Krause Publications
700 E. State St.
Iola, WI 54990-0001
snippetsensation@aol.com

All books, notions, and supplies mentioned and illus-
   trated in this book available through:
Eddie's Quilting Bee
264 Castro St.
Mountain View, CA 94041
1-888-QUILTER
www.Quilting bee.com

Notions supplied by:
American & Efird, Inc. (Mettler and Signature threads)
Coats & Clark (notions)
Fairfield Processing Corporation (batting)
Golden Threads (quilting line designs)
Gingher (scissors)
Gutermann of America (thread)
Hobbs (batting)
Husqvarna Viking Sewing Machine Company
Kelsul, Inc. Quilters Cotton Batting
LYI (thread)
Morning Glory (batting)
New Cities Designer Fabrics (Diana Leone's designs)
Northcott/Monarch Fabrics
Olfa Products
Omnigrid

Prym-Dritz Corporation
Springs OTC (Quilter's Only and Cindy Walter Snippet
   Designs)
Stearns (Mountain Mist Batting)
The Warm Company (Warm n' Natural batting, Steam-
   a-seam2 fusible web)
W.H. Collins (notions)
Wrights (EZ Notions)

Moonstone Creations
612 Lighthouse Ave., Ste. 217
Pacific Grove, CA 93950
www.quiltwoman.com

The Perfect Patchwork Templates
Marti Michell
3525 Broad Street
Chamblee, GA 30341
770-458-6500

Powell Publications
Quilting Line Design Books
8416 208th Ave. NE
Redmond, WA 98053
425-898-0332

Quilting Creations
International, Inc.
PO Box 512
Zoar, OH 44697
330-874-4741

StenSource International Inc.
18971 Hess Ave.
Sonora, CA 95370-9724

Thimbleberries, Inc.
205 Jefferson St.
Hutchinson, MN 55350